About 3300 hundred miles the wide of ...

NEW MEXICO COLO.
RATON PASS 8700 FEET
TRINIDAD

LA JUNTA	LAS ANIMAS	LAMAR	SYRACUSE CITY	GARDEN CITY	CIMARRON CITY	DODGE	KINSLEY	LARNED	GREAT BEND	McPHERSON	SALINA	JUNCTION CITY	TOPEKA	LAWRENCE	KANSAS CITY	ODESSA	COLUMBIA	ST. CHARLES	ST. LOUIS
22	37	55	54	34	19	39	25	24	65	37	54	80	27	46	44	94	105	21	

THIS ROAD IS "FREE"
IF BUSINESSMEN WHO ARE RECOMENDED ON THIS GUIDE CAN NOT SUPPLY SAME TO YOU WRITE TO "WHITE CAFE" GALLUP N. M.

SCALE OF MILES. 50 0 50 100

LOS ANGELES
GALLUP, N. M.
SANTA FE N. M.
TRINIDAD COL.
LA JUNTA COL.
DODGE CITY KAN.
McPHE...

KANSAS
MOUNTAIN TIME WEST OF

CENTER OF U.S.

Route 66 elevation / distance table:

Get a Copy of This Map WHITE CAFE GALLUP N. M.	White Cafe	Amarillo Hotel Rule Bldg. Garage	Tourist Cottage Camp	Lincoln Service Studio	GIBSON'S Service Station	K. C. Auto Hotel Nineck's Cafe	CHRISTMAN Cafeteria	HOSTON Coffee Shop	FELLOWS Auto Storage	The Peacock Food Shop BALTIMORE HOTEL	18th Street Garage Majestic Hotel Hotel Abraham Lincoln Wilk's Restaurant	Morrison Hotel

GALLUP 167 SANTA ROSA 173 TUCUMCARI 117 AMARILLO 163 ELK CITY 106 OKLAHOMA 29 CHANDLER 48 TULSA 73 VINITA 73 JOPLIN 62 SPRINGFIELD 73 LEBANON 73 ROLLA 54 CUBA 25 ST LOUIS 73 SPRINGFIELD 117 PONTIAC 95 JOLIET 61 CHICAGO 58

ELEVATION MILES DISTANCES

6000 5000 4000 3000 2000 1000 LEVEL

66

TEXAS OKLA.

OKLA.

D1217270

ROADSIDE AMERICA

365 DAYS

Lucinda Lewis

Harry N. Abrams, Inc., Publishers

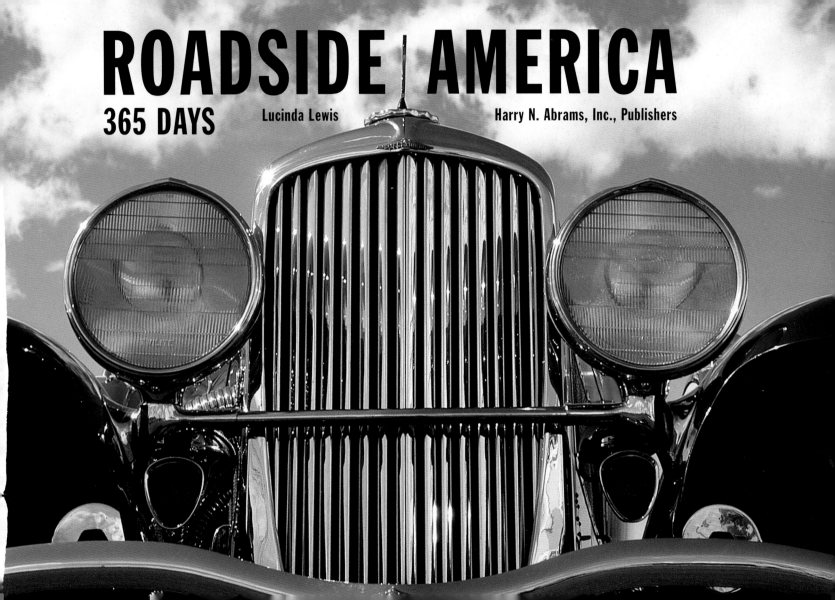

INTRODUCTION

As the nineteenth century metamorphosed into the twentieth, America was a nation on the move. Mobility was the centerpiece of the modern way. Widely regarded as a nation of tinkerers, the country turned its inventive spirit to the automobile in the 1890s. Early automotive designs featured varied sources of propulsion, and steam, gasoline, and electricity all had their proponents. The nascent automobile industry staged spectacular road-racing events to build publicity for its wares, which proved to be a great advertising device for inventors, Henry Ford among them.

Soon after their introduction, automobiles assumed a position they have held ever since—they conferred status. As toys for the rich, they segregated those with and without money at a glance. Much of the early status of automobiles resulted from their scarcity: from 1903 to 1904, only twenty-two Buicks were built! Unless you were a doctor, your motivation for buying an automobile was probably pure pleasure. But drivers soon discovered it was difficult and scary to operate the ill-smelling beasts while being enveloped in a cloud of dust or beaten up from the crude macadam beneath. Hats, goggles, dusters, driving gloves, and lap robes were necessary armor to face the joys and perils of the early highway.

Ford was eventually lured away from the racetrack and into production with a clear vision of the automobile he would build: "a car for the great multitude." He exclaimed, "It will be constructed of the best materials, by the best men to be hired, after the simplest designs that modern engineering can devise. But it will be low in price so that no man making a good salary will be unable to own one—and enjoy with his family the blessings of hours of pleasure in God's great open spaces." The introduction of the Model T in 1908 realized Ford's dream at the astonishingly low price of $850. With further efficiency measures on the assembly line, production increased and the price of the Model T dropped to an astounding $250 by 1922.

With reliable and affordable cars available at last, the middle classes took to the automobile in droves. In the 1910s it was still common to see horses pulling wagons alongside automobiles. This uneasy alliance continued until the early 1920s, when the horse finally yielded to the car. At first, proud new car owners were content to join the passing parade on Main Street. Soon, however, the lust for adventure began to unfurl on wings of its own. What lay beyond the outskirts of town? The Sunday drive into the countryside became a national pastime in the 1920s.

However, the development of well-marked and adequately paved roads lagged behind the demand for cars. By 1913 the Lincoln Highway Association had mapped a coast-to-coast route bisecting the nation, a 3,300-mile hodgepodge of connecting roads in various conditions. Although they could have taken the train, many travelers preferred the challenge of the highway (or lack thereof). Families loaded their vehicles and set off into the great unknown with a sense of exhilaration. These early transcontinental trips were acts of faith, great adventures that fostered a sense of community on the open road.

The Lincoln Highway broadened opportunities for coast-to-coast travel, but those wishing to travel to the Southwest still struggled against many odds. Highway authorities mapped Route 66 in 1926 by stringing together the National Old Trails Roads to form a continuous ribbon of blacktop from Chicago, Illinois, to Santa Monica, California. It was years, however, before the road was completely paved.

Prior to the completion of the "Main Street of America" and the rise of its roadside businesses, auto travelers frequently depended upon the fabled kindness of strangers, setting out armed only with their daring spirit and a few provisions. The new gas stations and garages serviced their mechanical conveyances, while tourist camps and cabins offered weary passengers shelter for the night.

Ironically, the 1929 stock market crash did little to deter Detroit from turning out cars in ever greater numbers. That year, the Ford Model A and the six-cylinder "Stovebolt" Chevrolet both made their debuts. Many people were willing to make sacrifices in order to own a car. Aiding in their decision was an advertising industry that was coming of age, honing its skill at promoting the car as a key to a better life. Practicality was a persuasive rationale for buying a car, but cars also assumed a social role: going for a ride became a form of entertainment. Americans took drives to cool off on hot summer evenings instead of relaxing on their front porches. Some critics even saw the car as a threat to moral standards when courting moved from the parlor to the back seat, and when all-day Sunday trips lured families from church pew to highway.

Although America developed a plan for a national highway system in 1925, it was almost 1940 before the dream became a reality and the highways were paved from coast to coast. Once a network of through-roads was in place, the country suddenly became smaller. Formerly lonely roadsides were transformed by the vital trinity of gas, food, and lodging. Family-owned diners and cafes became popular destinations for so-called home-cooked meals, and roadside lodgings—the first were campgrounds—sprang up in close proximity to these enterprises. Curiously, the Great Depression fueled the growth of roadside America. The Works Progress Administration provided jobs such as road paving for unemployed workers, and it was these improved roads that carried some destitute families westward to lands of greater opportunity.

As America shook off the Depression, the fallout from tough economic times caused many car manufacturers to cease production. Ironically, the automobile industry staggered just as roadside America was taking off. The boom began with establishments for servicing the car, running the gamut of major oil companies with streamlined moderne gas stations to independent dealers hawking the cheapest gas available. Stations competed for the motorist's attention with promotional giveaways, uniformed attendants, and quality of service. Restaurants, motels, and tourist attractions followed suit with larger-than-life visibility to draw in customers. The first fast-food franchises appeared in the 1930s, originating with the Steak 'n' Shake in St. Louis, Missouri, which expanded into a mighty chain of coveted hamburger stands across the Midwest.

The proliferation of roadside signs caused a demand for creative sign painters along Route 66 and other major highways. The first of the famous Burma Shave billboard series appeared in Minnesota in 1925; by the late 1930s the billboard concept was in full flower. Unlike eastern states, with their preexisting urban centers, the western states were a tabula rasa. They were entirely free to invent their own mythology along the new highways. Route 66 crossed some of the most romantic countryside in America. It soon became clear to entrepreneurs in the Southwest that the motifs of cowboys and Indians could be milked all the way to the bank. "Spend the night in a tepee" read the popular billboard promoting the famed Wigwam Village.

With the gasoline rationing of the World War II era, traffic and business across the America's highways slowed to a crawl. The routes began to transport not only military convoys but also manpower for the aviation industry developing in California. By 1942, Detroit was not building any cars: America had redirected all its mighty industries to the war effort. Roadside businesses accepted ration coupons and struggled to balance their accountings. Servicemen and their families were the principal customer base on the road.

After the war it became clear that the country's roads were inadequate. For one thing, the highways were too narrow for the postwar car designs. Dusting off a long-range planning survey from 1934, federal highway authorities devised a new interstate system. America's roadside was about to change again.

Roadside America retooled with the advent of big-time road advertising to appeal to the growing tourist trade. Motels began to feature swing sets, outdoor furniture, and private full baths in each room, then later cranked up the competition with more lavish amenities: a pool, TV, and air-conditioning chief among them. The seeds of commercial vernacular architecture that were sown in the 1930s germinated in the postwar boom, spawning new car-culture icons: restaurants with curbside service, drive-in movie theaters, and souvenir stands. Buildings were sometimes designed as giant versions of the products sold within, such as a hot-dog stand in the shape of a giant hot dog. This pop architecture style—known as programmatic architecture—reached its heyday in the 1950s, although it was used with less frequency into the 1970s.

During the 1950s, car culture moved into a full-tilt boogie: the car dictated our architecture, the way we ate, the way we lived, and the way we drove. Peace and prosperity brought gadgets galore, modern conveniences designed to part us from our expanding wealth. Detroit's dream of selling us a new car every year and putting two cars in every garage became a compelling imperative for many consumers. Each year, excited crowds congregated outside auto dealerships to witness the unveiling of the new car models.

In the early 1950s automotive design was quite restrained compared to the flamboyant forms at the decade's end. Manufacturers became locked in a fierce competition—an escalating look-at-me design philosophy that paralleled the cold war and the space race. One of the most recognizable manifestations of this mania was the introduction of tail fins, which grew and grew until they culminated in the outrageous 1959 Cadillac. Even commercial architecture was gravity defying: boomerangs, parabolas, swooping awnings, and atomic-style neon signs led us into the future as the full-blown development of "the strip" became a reality. The advent of air-conditioning killed the drive-in; instead, modern coffee shops flaunted their climate-controlled environments by integrating enormous plate-glass windows with soaring rooflines.

The new interstate highway system circumnavigated most of the colorful, mom-and-pop commercial strips that had sprouted along America's early routes. Major sections of Route 66 were bypassed, causing many once-vibrant establishments to close their doors. The new highways proved to be a mixed blessing for the motorist: traffic flow and travel times improved, but the trips were no longer as much fun.

With no commercial strip to distract us, we began to concentrate on horsepower. In the 1960s American car manufacturers started to feel the influence of European road-racing design as the exploits of a new breed of hero, the race-car driver, fueled our lust for speed. A new, low-slung design aesthetic shucked fifties chrome excesses in favor of lean styling and faster performance. The muscle car was born.

Road signs along the new interstates exemplified a new way of life. As the signs grew bigger—and easier to read at high speeds—the buildings they advertised became less interesting. The Highway Beautification Act of 1972 limited the number and size of highway signs. Roadside consumers would have to rely on generic signs indicating gas, food, and lodging franchises located at the EZ-on and EZ-off exits, with no chance to case the joint before pulling off the highway. Gone were the eccentric ad campaigns and the independently owned enterprises.

The gas crisis of the 1970s dramatically changed the automobile industry. Americans began to abandon Detroit's fuel-slurping monsters and gravitated toward Japanese economy cars. It took years for American manufacturers to engineer their way out of trouble and once again compete in the marketplace.

After the hard-won frugality of the 1970s and 1980s, falling gas prices in the 1990s caused Americans to return to an age of automotive exuberance. This time, the "bigger is better" philosophy manifested itself in the craze for sport utility vehicles, two-ton behemoths that swill fuel like hogs at the trough. However, as the twenty-first century begins, consumers are gradually confronting the reality that overconsumption of resources is fast becoming a critical issue. Once again, foreign manufacturers are leading the way, this time with the development of hybrid gas/electric engines and other technological advances geared to fuel efficiency.

On our overburdened highways, traffic is nearing the standstill of two-lane America in the 1920s. Today in Los Angeles it is entirely possible to spend an entire day without leaving the car. The dedicated Angeleno will leave the house in the morning with a cooler containing special treats not available at the drive-thru he will patronize. Errands to run? No problem—drive-thru cleaners, banks, and convenience stores have adapted themselves to our car-crazed world. E-mails and faxes enter the car through the cigarette lighter while we yak on our cell phones in five lanes of bumper-to-bumper traffic.

No matter what the future brings, the transcendental quality of the open highway still remains if you are willing to take the road less traveled.

JANUARY

1 2 3 4 5 6 7 8 9 10 11 12 13 14 15 16 17 18 19 20 21 22 23 24 25 26 27 28 29 30 31

With its distinctive center headlight, this 1948 Tucker Four-Door Sedan looks a little like an alien visitor. Actually, the Tucker was a brilliantly designed car, so far ahead of its time that it fell afoul of the powers that be in Detroit. The definitive film portrait of automaker Preston Tucker and the cars he created is Frances Ford Coppola's *Tucker, A Man and His Dream*.

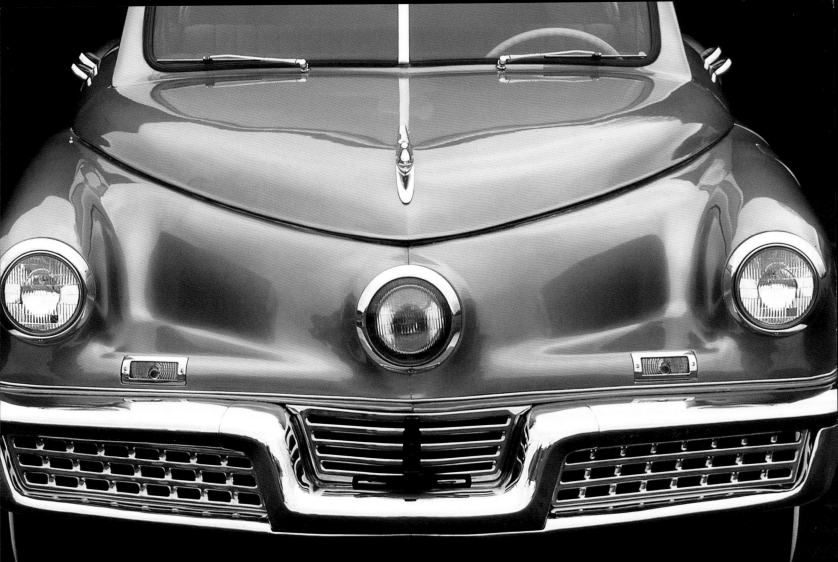

Rarely have things been cozier at the Cozy Drive-In in Netcong, New Jersey, than with this fleet of vintage lovelies tucked in side by side. Something about the rounded lines of these fifties favorites suggests comfort food—a frothy milkshake, a spattering hot burger, or a big basket of crispy fries with ketchup. These cars are all Chevrolets (models include the Bel Air, Corvette, Impala, Biscayne, and Malibu) with the exception of a Ford Crown Victoria and a Buick Riviera. Dating from 1955 to 1964, they provide an indelible record of automotive styling during those years.

JANUARY

1 2 **3** 4 5 6 7 8 9 10 11 12 13 14 15 16 17 18 19 20 21 22 23 24 25 26 27 28 29 30 31

Dinosaur

Cabazon, California

This blood-encrusted Tyrannosaurus (looking a little like a sentry from a 1950s Japanese horror flick) has given a thrill to generations of visitors at the Grand Canyon caverns. For this 1953 Cadillac Series 62 Coupe, designer Bill Mitchell modified the 1948 model with the toothy "Dagmar" front bumper, not unlike the grin of T-Rex behind.

Sales drops throughout the difficult Depression era and war years forced Packard to reevaluate its position as one of America's ultimate luxury cars. This postwar 1947 Packard Super Clipper was priced to allow more middle-income Americans to tour the country under the venerable Packard banner. The resulting profits were used to offset Packard's losses in the luxury limousine segment. Ultimately, the marketing plan caused Packard—America's only truly independent upscale manufacturer—to lose its cachet, and the company was forced to merge with Studebaker in 1954.

This 1914 Model T Roadster dates from the beginning of the Henry Ford legend. Already Ford's dictum of function over form is obvious. The round barn in the background reflects the same utilitarian philosophy: It was built in Oklahoma by a Dutch immigrant who thought the round shape would be resistant to windstorms. So far so good.

JANUARY

1 2 3 4 5 6 **7** 8 9 10 11 12 13 14 15 16 17 18 19 20 21 22 23 24 25 26 27 28 29 30 31

With growing public awareness of the automobile, the advertising image became crucial to new car sales. The first brand to capitalize on this phenomenon was the Jordan, which thrived on the motto "Somewhere, West of Laramie." Drivers got the message that they could depend on Jordans like this 1923 Playboy to traverse the vast spaces of the American West. This simple motto enticed a generation of consumers to take the plunge.

1 2 3 4 5 6 7 **8** 9 10 11 12 13 14 15 16 17 18 19 20 21 22 23 24 25 26 27 28 29 30 31

1909 Ford Model T Touring dashboard

JANUARY

1 2 3 4 5 6 7 8 **9** 10 11 12 13 14 15 16 17 18 19 20 21 22 23 24 25 26 27 28 29 30 31

Designed by Dr. Ferdinand Porsche for Mercedes Benz, the ultrafast SSK model created tremendous publicity. Built primarily for racing, the 1929 Mercedes Benz Sport Model SSK had one disconcerting flaw. At speed, it had difficulty in turns.

JANUARY

1 2 3 4 5 6 7 8 9 **10** 11 12 13 14 15 16 17 18 19 20 21 22 23 24 25 26 27 28 29 30 31

Dual horns balance the symmetrical headlights of this 1933 Chrysler Imperial Custom
Eight Phaeton with a body by Le Baron.

JANUARY

1 2 3 4 5 6 7 8 9 10 **11** 12 13 14 15 16 17 18 19 20 21 22 23 24 25 26 27 28 29 30 31

1933 Pierce Arrow Silver Arrow hood ornament

JANUARY

1 2 3 4 5 6 7 8 9 10 11 **12** 13 14 15 16 17 18 19 20 21 22 23 24 25 26 27 28 29 30 31

Designed by Gordon Buehrig for an honorary fireman, George Whittell, this 1933
Duesenberg Model SJ features a black-and-white paint job of unparalleled sophistication.
The two-tone treatment accentuates the sculptural beauty of the handwrought body
and attracted ample attention when Mr. Whittell drove it in parades.

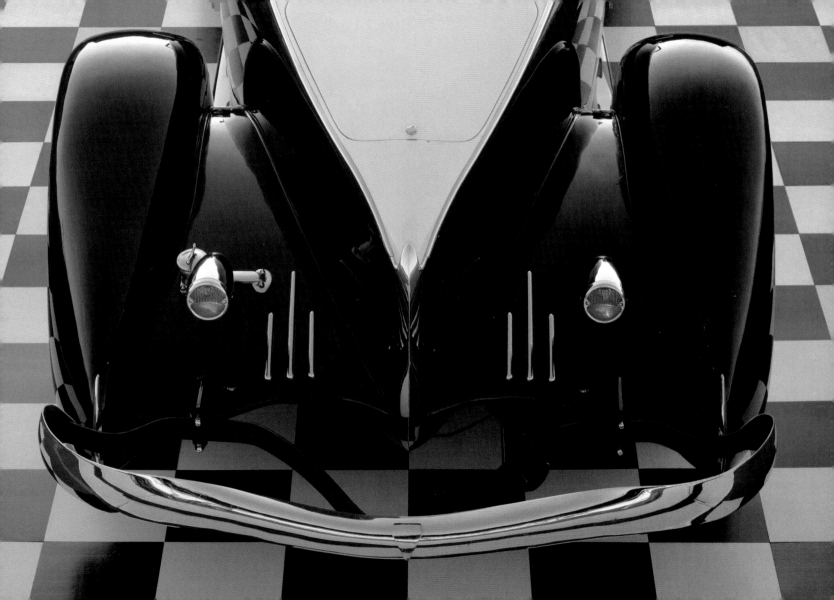

1921 Pierce Arrow door handle

JANUARY

1 2 3 4 5 6 7 8 9 10 11 12 13 **14** 15 16 17 18 19 20 21 22 23 24 25 26 27 28 29 30 31

Erret Loban Cord was a wheeler-dealer who enjoyed working the stock market as much as he did the design and manufacture of automobiles. In the automotive world, Cord remains one of America's most influential designers. He created his self-named company in the late 1920s to fill the gap between his medium-priced Auburn line and the top-flight Duesenberg. The Cord L-29 pictured here was one of the first cars ever built with front-wheel drive. This feature catapulted Cord to the forefront of automotive innovation. As is often the case with engineering breakthroughs, certain shortcomings became apparent. The car was slower than had been hoped for and handling was a little skittish in adverse conditions. Compensating for mechanical faults were the L-29's movie-star looks. Front-wheel drive allowed for a low, flowing style that made the Cord one of the most attractive cars of its own decade and any since.

JANUARY

1 2 3 4 5 6 7 8 9 10 11 12 13 14 **15** 16 17 18 19 20 21 22 23 24 25 26 27 28 29 30 31

The sturdy wooden wheel on this 1917 Cole Tourcoupe boasts of the car's claim to fame—
a V-8 engine.

The American need for speed was great. Chrysler's Hemi engine of the 1950s had kicked off the horsepower race, and the 1960s saw its culmination in this powerful engine, the 1969 Plymouth GTX Hemi.

For early-morning empire builders, Lou Mitchell's restaurant offers a breakfast of champions that has made it a Chicago legend. Just a few blocks from the origin of Route 66, Lou Mitchell's has seen many travelers filling up prior to the continental crossing. There is also a solid clientele of traders and other denizens of the nearby Chicago Board of Trade and Mercantile Exchange. This spectacular 1937 Cord 812 Supercharged Phaeton would be the ride of choice for a successful financier. Designed in 1936 by renowned stylist Gordon Buehrig, the Phaeton was revolutionary in its streamlined design and boisterous power. Mounted on the Cord's dash is a plaque guaranteeing that this particular model will go 110.8 mph. Truly a car for the City of the Big Shoulders, the Cord's Lycoming Supercharged V-8 engine, with 289 cubic inches and front-wheel drive, made it the fastest stock car produced prior to 1947.

Lou Mitchell's
Serving the worl finest COFFEE
This is Lou Mitchell's
RESTAURANT & BAKERY
We do our own Quality baking
Hand Made
BAKERY
Milk Duds
565
Hours

JANUARY

1 2 3 4 5 6 7 8 9 10 11 12 13 14 15 16 17 **18** 19 20 21 22 23 24 25 26 27 28 29 30 31

This revamped 1932 Ford Roadster is one of the original Mean Machines. The hot-rod movement sprung up in the 1950s in Southern California, where building your own personal fire-breathing monster made you a bona fide hepcat.

JANUARY

1 2 3 4 5 6 7 8 9 10 11 12 13 14 15 16 17 18 **19** 20 21 22 23 24 25 26 27 28 29 30 31

1933 Duesenberg Model SJ Speedster with a body by Schwartz

"It was a rich cream color, bright with nickel, swollen here and there in its monstrous length with triumphant hat-boxes and supper boxes and tool-boxes, and terraced with a labyrinth of windshields that mirrored a dozen suns."

F. SCOTT FITZGERALD, DESCRIBING JAY GATSBY'S CAR IN *THE GREAT GATSBY*

JANUARY

1 2 3 4 5 6 7 8 9 10 11 12 13 14 15 16 17 18 19 **20** 21 22 23 24 25 26 27 28 29 30 31

Irving Berlin's ode to unbridled optimism would be tragically undercut in a few short years by the Great Depression. Yet this 1929 Duesenberg Model J would sail on blithely.

"Blue skies smilin' at me, nothing but blue skies do I see . . ."

"BLUE SKIES," BY IRVING BERLIN, 1927

1 2 3 4 5 6 7 8 9 10 11 12 13 14 15 16 17 18 19 20 **21** 22 23 24 25 26 27 28 29 30 31

One of America's first luxury cars, the 1911 Crane Simplex 4-Passenger Tourabout was inspired by some of Europe's early vehicles. Believing that anything Europe could build, America could build better, the Simplex Motor Car Company entered automotive manufacture. The merger of Simplex with the Crane Motor Company, renowned for its engines, yielded outstanding luxury automobiles.

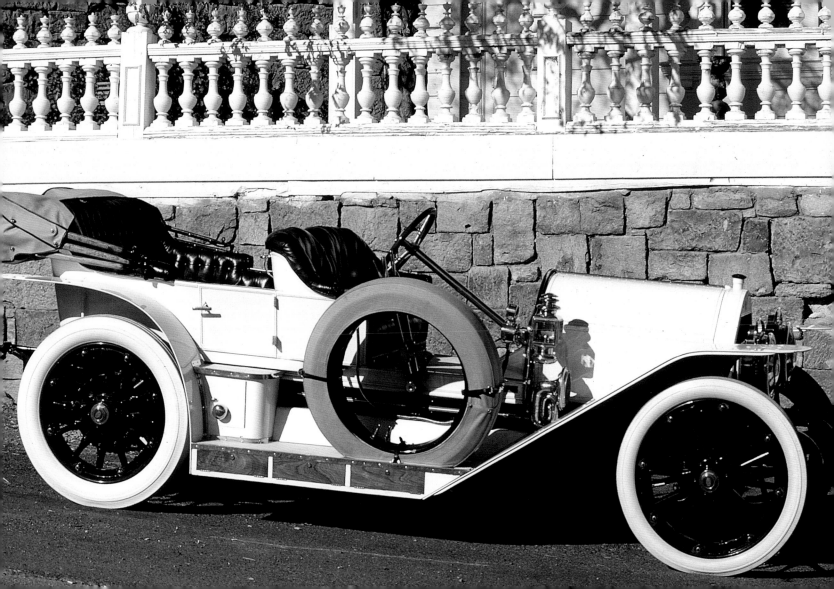

JANUARY

1 2 3 4 5 6 7 8 9 10 11 12 13 14 15 16 17 18 19 20 21 **22** 23 24 25 26 27 28 29 30 31

1950 Cadillac Series 61 Sedan

For the man with big dreams, the 1926 Jordan Playboy promised romance.

JANUARY

1 2 3 4 5 6 7 8 9 10 11 12 13 14 15 16 17 18 19 20 21 22 23 **24** 25 26 27 28 29 30 31

Once owned by Lana Turner, this head-turning bright orange 1941 Chrysler Newport
Dual Cowl Phaeton sports an elegant dashboard.

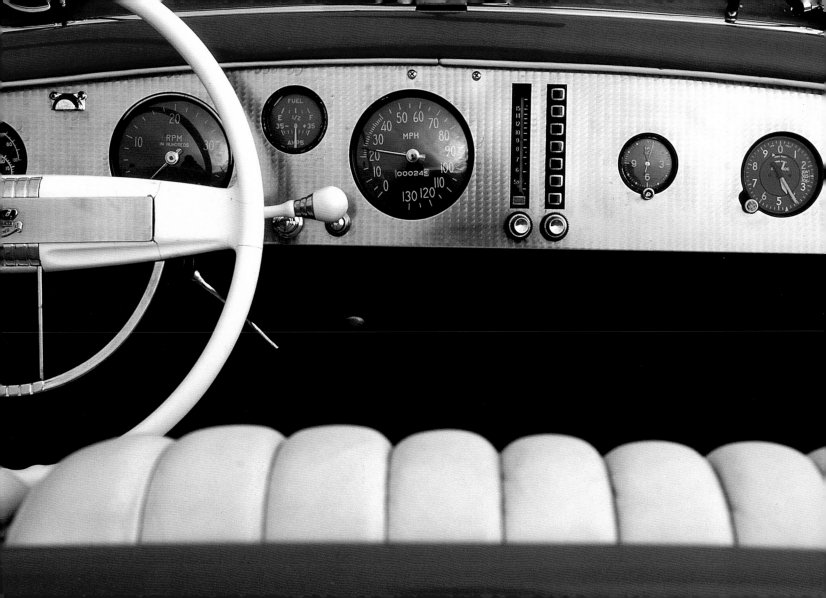

JANUARY

1 2 3 4 5 6 7 8 9 10 11 12 13 14 15 16 17 18 19 20 21 22 23 24 **25** 26 27 28 29 30 31

Close to the Edge
Marin Headlands, California

JANUARY

Automotive design in the early 1950s was restrained compared to the flamboyant look of the decade's end. As the years rolled by fierce competition in Detroit caused the auto designer to fixate on a "look at me" philosophy. Wider, lower, bigger, and zoomier culminated in outrageous tail fins, like those on this 1959 Buick Electra 225.

JANUARY

1 2 3 4 5 6 7 8 9 10 11 12 13 14 15 16 17 18 19 20 21 22 23 24 25 26 **27** 28 29 30 31

The call of the Dixie Truckers Home neon sign is hard for most semi drivers to resist while crossing Illinois.

DIXIE
TRUCKERS HOME

JANUARY

1 2 3 4 5 6 7 8 9 10 11 12 13 14 15 16 17 18 19 20 21 22 23 24 25 26 27 **28** 29 30 31

Still driven daily, this 1947 Studebaker pickup is a real workhorse on the owner's
New Mexico ranch.

And you thought all the leaning towers were in Pisa. In a consummate piece of high-plains architectural theater, the Britten water tower was deliberately created with one leg shorter than the others. As it is the only structure on the horizon, approaching motorists become fascinated by the irregularity, eventually questioning the very tilt of the horizon itself. This 1930 Ford Model A Flatbed truck is immune to the joke as it continues about its daily tasks with relentless purpose. Owned by the local proprietors of the Truck Terminal and Ranch House Cafe, this Model A has a history of hard work for its previous owners—it was first used to haul boilers off the oil fields, then to haul grain.

JANUARY

1 2 3 4 5 6 7 8 9 10 11 12 13 14 15 16 17 18 19 20 21 22 23 24 25 26 27 28 29 **30** 31

Who could forget the Colonel in his white suit and black string tie? More important, who could forget the bucket of delicious fried chicken he extolled? A large reproduction of that famous bucket spun atop every Kentucky Fried Chicken across America. But look for it today and you'll discover the bucket and the name "Kentucky Fried Chicken" have been replaced with the anonymous acronym KFC: an attempt to make us forget the word *fried*. As soon as we realized this metamorphosis was occurring, we rushed out to make this photograph. We decided the family-sized 1950 Chrysler Town & Country Newport was big enough to hold all the fried chicken we could eat (just barely).

JANUARY

1 2 3 4 5 6 7 8 9 10 11 12 13 14 15 16 17 18 19 20 21 22 23 24 25 26 27 28 29 30 **31**

This 1928 Chevrolet Pickup was marketed under the Chevrolet slogan "Bigger and Better." What could be more American? Chevrolet's six-cylinder engine was indeed larger than Ford's four-cylinder model. The slogan paid off: 1928 was the second year in a row where Chevrolet was no. 1 in sales.

FEBRUARY

1 2 3 4 5 6 7 8 9 10 11 12 13 14 15 16 17 18 19 20 21 22 23 24 25 26 27 28

San Francisco Bay area residents affectionately know this 1928 Packard Convertible
Coupe as the "Orange Crush."

As the 1960s dawned, Cadillac designers began streamlining the 1950s curves. While this 1960 Cadillac Sedan DeVille still has fins, they appear as afterthoughts to the tapering rear that recalls a turbine shape. An oversized windshield and delicate roof struts augment the lighter-than-air feeling of this very large vehicle. Similarly aerodynamic is the Diner Store, formerly Uncle Bob's Diner, in Flint, Michigan. Constructed of porcelain and stainless steel by the O'Mahony Company of New Jersey, this and other diners never served as working railroad cars, as is often believed. The sleek designs of such diners made them economical, enabling them to be built as single units and shipped to far-flung locations.

FEBRUARY

1 2 **3** 4 5 6 7 8 9 10 11 12 13 14 15 16 17 18 19 20 21 22 23 24 25 26 27 28

The scandal-ridden DeLorean automotive company delivered a gull-winged, Guigaro-
designed body that is still coveted by enthusiasts. Although the brushed stainless-steel
body on this 1983 DeLorean Coupe is striking and unique, it makes fender benders
a nightmare to repair.

FEBRUARY

1 2 3 **4** 5 6 7 8 9 10 11 12 13 14 15 16 17 18 19 20 21 22 23 24 25 26 27 28

1957 Scimitar All Purpose Sedan

SCIMITAR

1952 Chrysler Imperial Newport dashboard

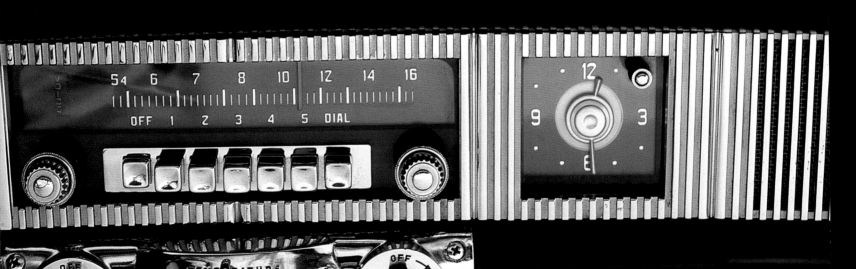

FEBRUARY

1 2 3 4 5 **6** 7 8 9 10 11 12 13 14 15 16 17 18 19 20 21 22 23 24 25 26 27 28

The parking lot of Al Mac's restaurant in Fall River, Massachusetts, is a buffet of colorful and tasty vintage delights. From left to right they are a 1957 Oldsmobile Super 88 Holiday Coupe, a 1957 Chevrolet Bel Air Sport Coupe, a 1958 Chevrolet Corvette Convertible, and a 1955 Chevrolet Bel Air Four-Door Sedan.

DINER
Al Mac's
RESTAURANT
JUSTLY FAMOUS SINCE 1910
OPEN
Les Desserts
KENNEDY JOHNSON '60

Nothing says "Southern California" quite as loud as a soft top and this sky blue 1964
Ford Thunderbird Convertible. By the mid-1960s, California led the world in the aerospace
industry. With a tail end tapering to brake lights that look like the glow of a jet's
afterburners, this T-Bird is a valentine to the sky-cowboys of the time. Advertising
referred to the "Thunderbird cockpit" and its "flight deck," which included a battery
of warning lights for malfunctions. Another California contribution to pop culture is the
Tail o' the Pup restaurant, whose programmatic architecture informs us instantly as
to its purpose. Built in 1946, the "Pup" remains a beloved fixture in its Los Angeles
neighborhood and in numerous films, where its appearance instantly signifies Lotus Land.

FEBRUARY

1 2 3 4 5 6 7 **8** 9 10 11 12 13 14 15 16 17 18 19 20 21 22 23 24 25 26 27 28

The enormous porcelain enamel and neon sign of the Westerner Motel in Seaside, California, is too much to resist for this 1968 Cadillac DeVille Convertible.

Hollywood came calling when location scouts chose the Big 8 Motel for Tom Cruise and Dustin Hoffman to play a crucial scene in the film *Rain Man* (1988). The motel's actual location in El Reno, Oklahoma, did not suit the story, necessitating the "Amarillo's Finest" sign, which proprietors have kept as a souvenir. Just as aggressive as the Big 8's signage is this 1968 Plymouth Road Runner, which was described as "the most brazenly pure and noncompromising super car in history" by *Motor Trend* magazine. Aimed at the "eat a burger, burn some rubber" crowd, the Road Runner was designed to accelerate to 100 mph within a quarter mile. You can almost smell the rubber and hear the squealing tires.

"In 1964, I loaded my wife and our two kids, ages four and two, into our unair-conditioned Plymouth Valiant for a journey from Washington, D.C. to Barstow, California. . . . As in pioneer days, I tried to drive 400 miles before stopping . . . four of us, two kids under four, in an unair-conditioned car on Route 66 in July. I felt like the wagonmaster trying to keep the renegade troops on the trail.

. . . It seemed as though we were on the trail for four months, but [it] was really four days. . . . We took the route that led across the cool Rockies through Denver back home. If we had tried Route 66, I would have been divorced and my kids would never have forgiven me to this day."

THE REV. BARRON MABERRY, WASHINGTON, D.C.

FEBRUARY

1 2 3 4 5 6 7 8 9 **10** 11 12 13 14 15 16 17 18 19 20 21 22 23 24 25 26 27 28

The Golden Gate Bridge looms high above this rare, low-slung 1980 BMW M1. Created at a time of corporate soul-searching, the M1 was BMW's bold effort to create a sports car that could run nose-to-nose with the Ferrari. Needless to say, it succeeded.

FEBRUARY

1 2 3 4 5 6 7 8 9 10 **11** 12 13 14 15 16 17 18 19 20 21 22 23 24 25 26 27 28

1933 Pierce Arrow Silver Arrow

In 1927, the Phillips Oil Company had created a new gasoline. The name for the new product was decided upon when two Phillips oil executives, traveling on Route 66, commented on how fast their car was going with the new Phillips gas. One said, "This car goes sixty with our new gas!" "Sixty nothing," said the other. "We're doing sixty-six." Upon hearing the story, owner Frank Phillips adopted "66" as part of the Phillips logo. Although the logo has gone through many design changes, "66" remains a proud part of the company history to this day.

This elegant sweep of chrome-trimmed glass graces the famous short-wheelbase 1935 Duesenberg SJ once owned by Gary Cooper. Widely recognized as a car for the super-rich, the Duesenberg failed to evolve with the times. With their powerful racing-bred engines, Duesenbergs suffered from a split personality when the custom-bodied cars were ordered with features catering to the genteel comfort of their affluent buyers. It was a bit of an anachronism for such a high-performance engine to be housed beneath town-car coachwork designed to tool city streets.

FEBRUARY

1 2 3 4 5 6 7 8 9 10 11 12 13 **14** 15 16 17 18 19 20 21 22 23 24 25 26 27 28

The Lagonda Series II and III startled the automotive world with its one-of-a-kind, love-it-or-hate-it styling. In comparison, this 1988 Aston Martin Lagonda Series IV was a refinement, boosting the number of headlights from four to six and featuring more rounded styling. Each V-8-powered car required 2,200 man-hours to assemble; they were produced at a rate of about one per week. This modern classic ceased production in January 1990.

FEBRUARY

1 2 3 4 5 6 7 8 9 10 11 12 13 14 **15** 16 17 18 19 20 21 22 23 24 25 26 27 28

Hairpin Curves
Oatman, Arizona

In the spring of 1929, the Grider family of four traveled from southwest Missouri to California on a 1929 Harley-Davidson motorcycle with a double-passenger sidecar:

"Route 66 was unpaved all the way. It took us seven days to reach Los Angeles at a total cost of $35. Campgrounds sometimes cost 25 cents; at times, we just camped by the road.

[My] wife and I and children, ages 3 and 1 year, took the following provisions and bought no food on the way: a seven-foot by seven-foot umbrella tent, four camp stools, washtub & board, two-burner gas stove for cooking and heat, two bedrolls, half-gal. ice cream freezer, two water bags, kerosene lantern for light, pressure cooker, aluminum kettle packed with pots, coffee pot & tableware, grocery box containing whole home-grown ham, flour, meal, eggs, jellies, Pet canned milk for gravy and bread making, and summer and winter clothing for four.

With the heavy load, the [Harley] would run 50 mph in high gear. I could out-run Greyhound buses on the dirt, washboard road. Most cars of that day could hardly make the grade at Oatman Pass northeast of Needles, California, but the cyclin' Griders made it in second gear fully loaded."

JOHN GRIDER, GREENFIELD, MISSOURI

The 1996 Dodge Viper GTS is the performance-coupe version of the high-profile Dodge Viper. The eight-liter V-10 engine underneath the hood of the sleek body is the reason why the Viper is *the* American sports car.

It is obviously hot-rod night at the Degadillo Snow Cap Cafe in Seligman, Arizona. This customized 1923 Model T Roadster flashes past its more domesticated brethren, the 1955 Chevrolet Bel Air, the 1967 Pontiac GTO Convertible, the 1957 Chevrolet Bel Air, and the 1966 Ford Mustang Convertible. The signage leads us to wonder what kind of patrons induced the "keep feet & hands off wall" prohibition.

No single technological innovation did as much to kill our drive-in culture as air-conditioning. Here cruising the local Dog 'n' Suds drive-in is a 1953 Buick Special.

1957 Packard Clipper Country Sedan hood ornament

More than just a meal in itself, this 1955 Cadillac Fleetwood 8 Passenger Sedan is a lavish feast for everybody in the vicinity. With enough room for the whole family, the Fleetwood 8 could fit grandparents and even a few step-relatives. Part of a limited production run, this car was used mostly as a limousine. It's similar to the formal Fleetwood Limousine Morgan Freeman used to chauffeur Jessica Tandy in the movie *Driving Miss Daisy*. Long famous for its hot dogs smothered in French fries and "sport" peppers (that's hot, to the uninitiated), Henry's in Cicero, Illinois, has been satisfying Route 66 customers since 1950. Also satisfying to Route 66 drivers is the Fleetwood 8's "Dagmar" bumper, named in a salute to Dagmar, the buxom hostess of Jerry Lester's *Tonight* show.

The "comet" in the sky above this 1956 Ford Fairlane Victoria is a rare period neon sign at the Comet Lanes in Grand Rapids, Michigan. The sign memorializes the glory of bowling's finest hour with "chase lights" (bulbs that flash on and off in sequence), which mimic the path of a bowling ball hitting pins. Bowling was promoted as a social activity in the suburbs springing up all over America in the mid-1950s. With cross-generational and multiethnic appeal, bowling was a sport everybody could enjoy: it brought social cohesiveness and fun to the melting pot that was suburban life in America at the time.

FEBRUARY

1 2 3 4 5 6 7 8 9 10 11 12 13 14 15 16 17 18 19 20 21 **22** 23 24 25 26 27 28

A Packard wheel. At the turn of the last century, embellished wooden spokes celebrated the wheel and its newly motorized revolutions.

One of a series of pre–Model T cars built by Henry Ford, the 1905 Ford Model C featured a left-side entrance for passengers. In the pre-T days, all Fords were right-hand drive, forcing passengers to enter and exit from the left into the frequently muddy streets. Right-hand drive allowed the driver to see how close he was to the edge of the road, but it was also a holdover from an earlier horseback tradition. Strangers on horseback always approached each other on the right, with their rifle barrels resting in the crooks of their left arms. This made it easier to defend themselves by pulling the trigger with the right finger, if need be.

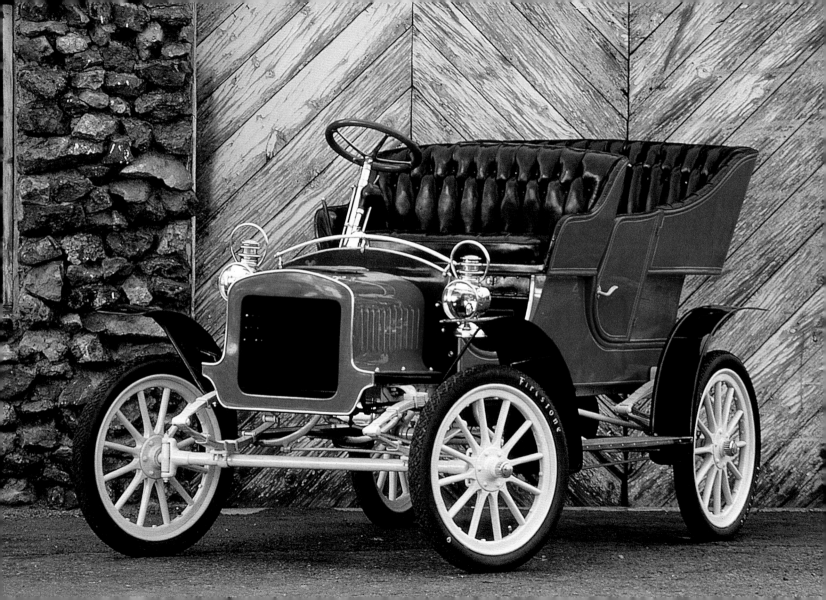

FEBRUARY

1 2 3 4 5 6 7 8 9 10 11 12 13 14 15 16 17 18 19 20 21 22 23 **24** 25 26 27 28

1927 Stutz Black Hawk Speedster

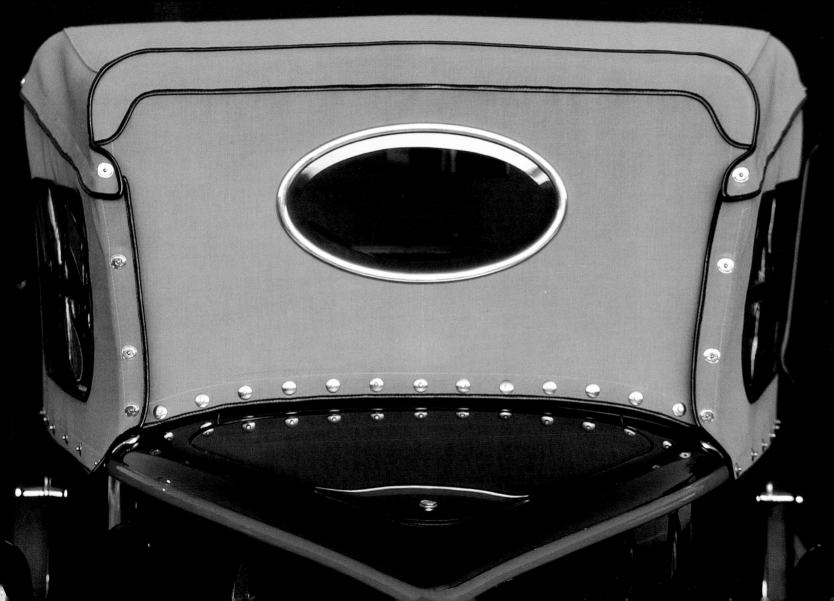

FEBRUARY

1 2 3 4 5 6 7 8 9 10 11 12 13 14 15 16 17 18 19 20 21 22 23 24 **25** 26 27 28

Crossing America's wide, open spaces in one's trusty 1922 Ford Model T Runabout was not a trip for the fainthearted.

A 1907 Success Model B Auto Buggy. There's something delightful about the utter simplicity of this arrangement: a wheel, hand brake, seat, steering wheel, and, most important of all, a large bulbous horn to blast others out of your way.

FEBRUARY

1 2 3 4 5 6 7 8 9 10 11 12 13 14 15 16 17 18 19 20 21 22 23 24 25 26 **27** 28

1957 Chevrolet Corvette

FEBRUARY

1 2 3 4 5 6 7 8 9 10 11 12 13 14 15 16 17 18 19 20 21 22 23 24 25 26 27 **28**

A real shark among muscle cars, the 1970 Plymouth Barracuda has a "Shaker" hood that reveals the Hemi engine's special air scoop.

The first four-wheel-drive Porsche raised the engineering bar for other manufacturers looking to enter the sports-car market. With its speed-deployed wing and new all-wheel drive, the 1989 Porsche Carrera 4 overcame torque problems caused by the trademark 911 rear-mounted engines.

The long-distance driver of this 1931 Ford Model A Deluxe Phaeton probably regarded this simple filling station as a life-sustaining oasis after the ordeal of the as-yet-untamed highway. Nonetheless, an eager public took to the new roads being built across America with unbridled enthusiasm. Witness the record set in 1930 by Charles Creighton and James Hargis: leaving New York on July 26, 1930, they drove their 1929 Ford Model A roadster *in reverse* to Los Angeles and back, covering 7,180 miles in forty-two days.

"In 1933, while driving a Model A Ford, the constant shaking loosened a jet in the carburetor and gasoline poured out of the bottom. I couldn't find the lost jet, but [I] fashioned a plug out of cork to stop the leak. Somehow the car ran with the cork plug as well as with the jet. On the same trip, near Gallup, New Mexico, about 200 feet of the road was under water as the result of a flash flood. Several cars were lined up at each side of the underwater portion. An Indian on horseback was nearby. I gave him a quarter to ride through before me so I could judge the depth of the water. At one point the water was so deep that the fan belt threw water on the spark plugs, which then shorted out. After drying them, I threw a flannel shirt over them to keep them dry. We finally made it safely with the other cars following me."

WILLIAM H. SHALLENBERGER, OXNARD, CALIFORNIA

Electric automobiles may be electrifying news today, but did you know they were running about in 1912? Featuring a tiller-style steering wheel, whisper-quiet operation, and an elegant cut-glass flower vase in the passenger compartment, the 1912 Baker Electric Runabout must have been a hit with the ladies.

MARCH

The cut-crystal bud vase found in this 1911 Franklin Limousine may have been the inspiration for the retro bud vase found in the Volkswagen New Beetle. Franklin, an early arrival on the automotive manufacturing scene, was known for its upscale air-cooled motorcars.

1928 Packard Convertible Coupe door handle

We've all heard that things are bigger in Texas, but the hood ornament on this 1960 Cadillac Series 62 Convertible gives new meaning to the phrase. These longhorns add a rakish touch to the otherwise restrained Caddy, with its especially large wraparound windshield. Equally outrageous is the challenge at the Big Texan Steak Ranch, which restores drama to the high plains by offering a free 72-ounce steak to anybody who can finish it in a one-hour sitting.

MARCH

1 2 3 4 5 6 **7** 8 9 10 11 12 13 14 15 16 17 18 19 20 21 22 23 24 25 26 27 28 29 30 31

There was a time when going topless might refer to driving your convertible—perhaps this modified 1927 Ford Model T Track Roadster. The car's mechanical simplicity and integrity made it readily adaptable to all kinds of modification.

MARCH

1 2 3 4 5 6 7 **8** 9 10 11 12 13 14 15 16 17 18 19 20 21 22 23 24 25 26 27 28 29 30 31

Best Bellies
Los Angeles, California

If you find yourself passing through Wilmington, Illinois, on Route 66, be sure to stop by the Launching Pad Café for a cup of coffee. The giant rocketman standing just outside will surely attract your attention. You can't miss it.

Young moguls have to start somewhere, and this 1993 Honda Civic Coupe offered higher quality and reliability at a lower price than most Detroit cars could muster at the time. With their low profile and surprising performance, many economy cars allow their drivers to enjoy pushing the speed limit, while flashier sports-car drivers tend to elicit the wrath of the police.

Breakdown
Mojave Desert, Arizona

"My second trip down 66 was in 1945. My husband and I retraced the [first] route, this time from L.A. to Kentucky. . . . As it was shortly after the war, there were many things that were still unavailable. Among these were tires. Because we couldn't buy new tires, we had all four tires recapped, plus the spare. We lost the caps to all five tires.

Cars were not air-conditioned so we bought an outside tank that was fastened to the outside of the window and blew air on you. It made so much noise that conversation was impossible . . . and [it] gave everyone the sniffles. Forgetting it was sticking out from the car, we drove too close to a post, hitting the air-conditioner and breaking the window.

After that, we bought a canvas bag in case the car overheated or we needed a drink of water. We tied it to the handle of the door on the driver's side. After a few miles, we discovered that the bag had swung back and forth and the metal top of the canvas bag had scraped off all the paint on the driver's side door. The trip cost us five tires, a window, and a paint job."

BOBBIE GORDON, GLENDALE, CALIFORNIA

With the two-lane blacktop stretching all the way to the horizon, this 1960 Chevrolet
Corvette Convertible is the ultimate open-road car for the ultimate open-road highway—
Route 66.

MARCH

This Nash Ambassador is an intrepid guest on gleaming Fremont Street in Las Vegas. Built for a generation of salesmen, the Ambassador features a back seat that folds down to provide a sleeping area for those so full of entrepreneurial spirit and thrift that they can't bear laying out money for a motel.

MARCH

1 2 3 4 5 6 7 8 9 10 11 12 13 **14** 15 16 17 18 19 20 21 22 23 24 25 26 27 28 29 30 31

The glitter gulch of Fremont Street in Las Vegas is a brilliant setting for the top-of-the-line
1959 Cadillac Eldorado Biarritz Convertible Coupe. Once the cruisin' heart of Vegas,
Fremont Street has since been remodeled into a domed pedestrian mall featuring an
overhead laser light show.

MARCH

In Albuquerque, New Mexico, Route 66 becomes Central Avenue and leads right past one of the town's most famous institutions, the El Vado Motel. With its Indian neon sign and classic Southwestern adobe architecture, the El Vado has provided safe haven for generations of 66 travelers. The famed motor court has operated almost continuously since its opening in 1937.

Like the spectacular New Mexico desert that surrounds it, the Blue Swallow Motel's pink- and-red-hot neon draws travelers like an exotic flower. The "Blue Swallow" logo and gleaming green "refrigerated air" promise cool, clean lodgings amid the blazing desert of surrounding Tucumcari. Designed in 1942, the Blue Swallow was recognized by the National Register of Historic Places as a prime example of early motel design. Equally classic is this ivory-white 1949 Chrysler Windsor. Although the car was produced after World War II, it reflects the prewar functional design ethic. For example, the Windsor is designed so a gentleman would not be forced to remove his hat when entering the car. The sun visor and architectural front grille set off the Windsor as a paragon of middle-American respectability.

MARCH

1 2 3 4 5 6 7 8 9 10 11 12 13 14 15 16 **17** 18 19 20 21 22 23 24 25 26 27 28 29 30 31

With its fluid ivory hood and golden wood sides, this 1940 Packard Custom Station Wagon is the perfect car for the gentleman farmer. The wood sides proclaim an affinity for the rural life while the meticulous grace of the limousinelike hood could pass muster at any gathering of automotive thoroughbreds.

MARCH

In the early 1960s, American auto manufacturers began to show the influence of European road racing in their designs. The exploits of a new breed of American hero fueled our attention to speed: the race-car driver. Major American racers of the day—such as Phil Hill, Carroll Shelby, and Richard Petty—became household names. Shelby went on to manufacture speed-tuned automobiles like this 1965 AC Shelby Cobra 427 SC.

MARCH

1 2 3 4 5 6 7 8 9 10 11 12 13 14 15 16 17 18 **19** 20 21 22 23 24 25 26 27 28 29 30 31

The crossed racing flags mounted on the side of this 1963 Chevrolet Corvette Stingray
Coupe are appropriate for such a fast car.

1933 Pierce Arrow Silver Arrow front

The swiveling driver's seat of the 1959 Dodge Custom Royal Lancer Convertible

Long before the retractable convertible Mercedes SLK wowed the automotive world there was this mechanical marvel. The Skyliner is the world's first mass-produced retractable hardtop, employing seven reversible electrical motors, ten power relays, twelve limit switches, and 654 feet of electrical cable to retract the entire hardtop into the trunk. What a show! This 1958 Ford Fairlane Skyliner Retractable includes the 352 V-8 Interceptor engine, factory air, power steering, and power bakes. The Skyliner Motel, located at the intersection of Route 66 and Route 99 in Stroud, Oklahoma, has been a popular overnight stop due in no small part to its enormous neon sign. This is one of the very few porcelain signs still standing in America.

From 1955 through 1957, Chevrolet incrementally refined its prized tail fin. The result is a restrained purity of form that made the 1957 Chevrolet Bel Air the quintessential 1950s car for many Americans.

1 2 3 4 5 6 7 8 9 10 11 12 13 14 15 16 17 18 19 20 21 22 23 **24** 25 26 27 28 29 30 31

Famed Italian designer Bertone built this swooping 1954 Alfa Romeo B.A.T. car.

The Welch brothers, classic American tinkerers, began experimenting with automobiles in 1901 from the back of a bicycle shop in Chelsea, Michigan. By 1909, this four-cylinder motor marked the pinnacle of their engineering: 50 horsepower.

MARCH

1 2 3 4 5 6 7 8 9 10 11 12 13 14 15 16 17 18 19 20 21 22 23 24 25 **26** 27 28 29 30 31

If you are into thrill rides, consider the 1957 Chevrolet Corvette as a worthy alternative to the "Giant Dipper" wooden roller coaster on the Santa Cruz, California, boardwalk.

The design of the 1957 Lincoln Premier Four-Door Sedan was typical of the exuberant decoration found on American cars in the finned era. Equally buoyant is the Uniroyal Tire, a fitting tribute to the Motor City. The 80-foot tire began life as a Ferris Wheel—it was Uniroyal's entry in the 1964 New York World's Fair. After the fair, the gondolas were replaced by simulated tread and the tire was relocated outside Detroit on Interstate 94, where it has become a famous landmark.

The 1964 Pontiac GTO Convertible became a legend the minute it hit the streets. A closely guarded secret for a year before its introduction, the GTO was the brainchild of GM's John DeLorean and Jim Wangers. The moment this baby's dual exhaust pipes rattled windows, the secret was out: its optional 389-cubic-inch, V-8 "Tri-Power" engine launches it from 0 to 60 mph in 4.6 seconds. Every bit as assertive as the GTO is this towering donut— a landmark on the L.A. skyline that's built 30 feet high to attract Angelenos from the nearby 405 freeway. Once called the Big Donut (how'd they come up with that one?), Randy's Donuts is now known as the "Mecca of dunkin'" and claims to be the world's first fast-food drive-in.

MARCH

1 2 3 4 5 6 7 8 9 10 11 12 13 14 15 16 17 18 19 20 21 22 23 24 25 26 27 28 **29** 30 31

Many movie palaces have gone the way of drive-ins and other roadside dinosaurs,
but the Wilson Theater in Fresno, California, survives intact, as does this 1968
Chevrolet Z28 Camaro.

MARCH

1 2 3 4 5 6 7 8 9 10 11 12 13 14 15 16 17 18 19 20 21 22 23 24 25 26 27 28 29 **30** 31

The distinctive 1957 Corvette became one of motordom's most coveted collectible automobiles.

M A R C H

1 2 3 4 5 6 7 8 9 10 11 12 13 14 15 16 17 18 19 20 21 22 23 24 25 26 27 28 29 30 **31**

Shakes

St. Louis, Missouri

At Steak 'n' Shake, hamburgers are steakburgers and every shake is hand-dipped. Founded in the 1930s with the slogan "in sight it must be right," the Steak 'n' Shake chain features steak ground into hamburger before the eyes of salivating patrons along with a guaranteed wait time of less than five minutes. Here, the Springfield, Missouri, Steak 'n' Shake hosts the Classic Chevy Club with curbside service.

STEAK n SHAKE
E CHILI
TRU-FLAVOR SHAKES
GRINDING ONLY GOV'T INSPECTED BEEF FOR STEAKBURGERS
ASAK
TAKHOMASAK
STEAK n SHAKE
It's a Meal

In the early 1980s Japanese automakers, full of confidence from the success of their economy cars in the marketplace, decided to enter the American luxury market with the introduction of the Acura, Lexus, and Infiniti lines. This 1987 Acura Legend coupe was the first luxury model from the Honda-owned Acura Corporation. The styling is notable for its clean, classic lines.

With the success of the Ford Model T, the Model A, and the V-8, Henry Ford was on a roll unmatched by any automobile manufacturer today. It is ironic that in the midst of this fabulous popularity the company should begin to lose its dominance of the market, but it did. GM and Chrysler were nipping at the heels of the aging Henry Ford, and by the close of World War II they had wrested the bulk of the market from Ford. Nevertheless, the addition of the V-8 engine to this classic 1935 Ford ½-ton pickup helped reinvigorate sales.

If the hustle and bustle of modern life gets to be too much, consider some time travel courtesy of Las Vegas's Luxor Hotel. Located just a block from the "Statue of Liberty" on the famed Vegas Strip, the Luxor re-creates the era when pharaohs ruled the Nile. If Cleopatra were alive today, we believe she would travel the Strip in style with this 1966 Cadillac Coupe DeVille Convertible as her royal barge. The famous Cadillac fins of the 1950s were reined in from their outrageous heights under design chief Harley Earl, who retired in 1958. Earl's successor, Bill Mitchell, steered Cadillac into tighter styling that featured less chrome and a more chiseled appearance. This streamlined austerity found popular acclaim as America became obsessed with the space race and the clean lines of space-age design. At 0 to 60 mph in ten seconds and with near-silent performance at a top speed of 140 mph, this Caddy beats a camel any day.

APRIL

1 2 3 4 **5** 6 7 8 9 10 11 12 13 14 15 16 17 18 19 20 21 22 23 24 25 26 27 28 29 30

Like a desert wind, this 1989 silver Porsche 911S has speed, grace, and mystery.
The double bubble over the convertible roof gives this car the smooth lines of a mirage.

The Tucker's advanced engineering is reflected in this rear view of the 1948 Tucker Four-Door Sedan. Elements of its design predate many of the space-age styling motifs that would become common in later decades.

APRIL

1 2 3 4 5 6 **7** 8 9 10 11 12 13 14 15 16 17 18 19 20 21 22 23 24 25 26 27 28 29 30

This 1993 Jeep Wrangler resembles the original military vehicle used in World War II. Perhaps because its utilitarian lines look ever ready for off-road activity, the Wrangler became a coveted urban symbol in the anything-can-happen 1990s.

APRIL

1 2 3 4 5 6 7 **8** 9 10 11 12 13 14 15 16 17 18 19 20 21 22 23 24 25 26 27 28 29 30

1902 Ford "999" engine

APRIL

1 2 3 4 5 6 7 8 9 10 11 12 13 14 15 16 17 18 19 20 21 22 23 24 25 26 27 28 29 30

1930 Franklin Pursuit grille

APRIL

1 2 3 4 5 6 7 8 9 **10** 11 12 13 14 15 16 17 18 19 20 21 22 23 24 25 26 27 28 29 30

1930 Duesenberg Model J Phaeton

Could the famous flying lady that graces the hood of many Rolls Royces have been the inspiration for this 1933 Cadillac mascot?

This 1985 example of the Ferrari GTO is powered by a 400-horsepower, twin-turbo V-8. Maximum speed is 190 mph. Only 272 examples of the car were produced. A recounting of its mere statistics cannot approach the sublime state elicited from driving such a sophisticated machine. To experience is to believe—and perhaps go into debt.

One of the last of the dual-cowl automobiles, this 1941 Chrysler Newport Dual Cowl Phaeton was specially trimmed for its appearance as an Indianapolis Speedway pace car. Cars like this one helped create an aura for the entire Chrysler line. Just look at those swooping fenders.

APRIL

1 2 3 4 5 6 7 8 9 10 11 12 13 **14** 15 16 17 18 19 20 21 22 23 24 25 26 27 28 29 30

The untouched landscape of the Laguna Indian Reservation stretches for miles through the New Mexico desert, traversed by the Rio Puerco River. Roadrunners and other wildlife thrive on this reservation, where the spirit of the Apache runs strong. Equally pristine are the lines of this pale blue 1957 Thunderbird Convertible. Predating the modern comforts of the 1950s (dubbed "the era of excess and accessories"), the Thunderbird recalls a leaner approach to motoring.

APRIL

1 2 3 4 5 6 7 8 9 10 11 12 13 14 **15** 16 17 18 19 20 21 22 23 24 25 26 27 28 29 30

Juan Degadillo of Seligman, Arizona, started the Degadillo Snow Cap Cafe in 1953 to cater to the thousands of tourists who flooded Route 66 in the postwar boom. The earliest menu just featured ice cream but, of course, folks wanted sandwiches too, so Juan, an incurable practical joker, added his famous "Dead Chicken Sandwiches," "Cheeseburgers with Cheese," and "Male and Female Sandwiches."

APRIL

1 2 3 4 5 6 7 8 9 10 11 12 13 14 15 **16** 17 18 19 20 21 22 23 24 25 26 27 28 29 30

Throughout the years, Henry's Hot Dog in Cicero, Illinois, has managed to keep its many steady clients happy. Henry dogs feature all the classic garnishes plus "sport," or hot peppers. They are topped with a mountain of French fries, hence the neon sign design and slogan "It's a meal in itself!"

In the late 1950s, Robert J. Lee heeded the advice, "Go west, young man," and packed his bags for Amarillo, Texas. He imagined a romantic life on the range, with cowboys and herds of cattle, but was disappointed to find that much of the flavor of old Texas had vanished. Believing other travelers would be disappointed as well, he founded the Big Texan Steak Ranch in 1960 on old Route 66, just outside of Amarillo. The theme was the Wild West, complete with gunslingers, cattle drives, and beef—lots and lots of beef. One day a skinny cowboy wandered in, declaring he was so hungry he "could eat the whole cow." Mr. Lee took him at his word and served him all the steak he could eat. Four pounds (or sixty-four ounces) later the cowpoke keeled over, and a great marketing idea was born. Mr. Lee began advertising "Free 72-oz. steak if eaten in one hour." In thirty-seven years, 27,158 people have attempted the feat, but only about one in six (or 4,514 folks) have succeeded. Visitors to the Big Texan can read the Rules of Engagement before tangling with the huge steak in the restaurant lobby. In a chuck wagon full of ice, you can examine your entire meal prior to ingestion, just to make sure your eyes are not bigger than your stomach. Today, the Big Texan is located alongside Interstate 40. In addition to the steak house, there is an adjacent motel featuring a Texas-shape swimming pool. It is still a family operation, with Mr. Lee's descendants running the show.

This 1948 Chrysler Town & Country is a classic woody wagon with a twist. Owner Leo Carillo crowned the front grille with a beguiling hood ornament. When you honk the horn, the car moos!

Before the current SUV craze, the pickup truck was a strictly utilitarian vehicle. For its time, this snazzy 1937 Reo Speed Delivery Pickup was unusual because it demonstrated that trucks were also capable of stylish good looks.

The famed Wigwam Village located on Route 66 in Holbrook, Arizona, is a prime example of Route 66 architecture at its finest. Three Wigwam Villages exist today, all built in the forties and fifties from the original blueprints of architect Frank Redford. His fee? The proceeds from the coin-operated radios located beside every bed. Beside the wigwams, from front to back, are a 1960 Chevrolet Corvette, a 1950 Mercury Four-Door Sedan, a 1961 Cadillac Series 63, and a 1966 Ford Thunderbird.

Lovingly restored by the original owner's family to its 1950s condition, the Wigwam Village in Holbrook, Arizona, features fifteen concrete wigwams with vintage woven-birch furniture and tiny fez-shape lampshades gracing tepeelike lamps.

"I remember that one of the highlights of each day's travel was the selection of a motel. In the 1950s, most motels on Route 66 were still small, independently run operations of unknown quality. Selecting one was not a decision to be made lightly. . . . As my mother slowly drove along the main street, [we] three kids gave a running evaluation of the motels: 'swings and slides,' 'looks crummy,' 'that one has a restaurant.' 'Oohh! A swimming pool! Probably too expensive, but can we, Mom?'

Narrowing our choices down to the top two or three, we made a second pass, stopping at each of the likely candidates. If the general consensus still prevailed after an external inspection, my mother would ask to see one of the rooms. In time, we got very good at this ritual, and rarely ended up in a place we didn't like.

I'm sure it is because of those experiences that I tend to seek out state highways over interstates and small motels over the chain giants when I travel with my own family. . . . We still drive slowly down the main street while my kids call out an evaluation of each motel. ('Oohh, Dad. A swimming pool and cable!')"

CHRIS CAVETTE, FREMONT, CALIFORNIA

An essential part of the Chrysler Corporation's renaissance, the LH platform's cab-forward design succeeded in increasing cabin volume without adding to a car's overall length. This 1993 Concorde is the luxury member of the LH family.

1 2 3 4 5 6 7 8 9 10 11 12 13 14 15 16 17 18 19 20 21 22 **23** 24 25 26 27 28 29 30

The NSX is Japan's answer to the exotic European high-performance sports car. Acura's
approach is one of ultra-efficiency. Its aluminum-alloy body and structure weigh forty
percent less than its steel counterpart, yet is just as strong. It has a mid-engine,
three-liter, DOHC, 24-valve V-6 that produces 270 horsepower, making it one of the
highest output-per-displacement production engines in the world.

Ford Mustang badge

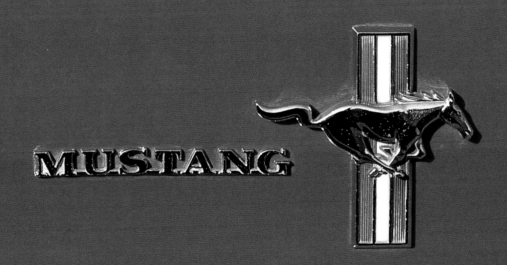

APRIL

1 2 3 4 5 6 7 8 9 10 11 12 13 14 15 16 17 18 19 20 21 22 23 24 **25** 26 27 28 29 30

The Art Deco–inspired Chrysler logo, circa 1940

1968 ½ Ford Mustang Cobra Jet interior

Have you met that special someone? Are you yearning to be united forever? Want to avoid unnecessary family drama? In short, are you ready to tie that knot *right now?* If so, we suggest a trip to Las Vegas's hub of happy matrimony—the Chapel of the Bells. However, this mint-condition Chevrolet Camaro Z28 Rally Sport might be destined more for the Fun City Motel at left. This is a classic muscle car whose form of seduction is speed. Chevrolet weighed in with the Camaro two years after Ford originated the Mustang: it was an instant hit. The Camaro's impressive power provided weekend racers lucky enough to own one with many a speedy thrill.

You can get pretty hot behind the wheel of a fast-moving Betty like this 1968 Shelby GT500 KR (that's for King of the Road). Designer Carroll Shelby's princely convertible is actually a fish-out-of-water in Vegas: it is one of only 318 built with the California surfboard option, which featured a surfboard tie-down mounted on the roll bar and, in keeping with the car's attention to detail, an actual surfboard color-coordinated with the car and boasting a trademark Shelby racing stripe. Nestled in pink stucco since 1956, the novelty portholes in the pool of the Glass Pool Inn accentuate the luxury of cooling off with an aquatic plunge in the parched desert heat.

Glowing taillights in the mile-wide fins of the 1960 Cadillac Fleetwood Model 60 Special Four-Door Sedan create an otherworldly feeling, as if the car might be an alien vehicle.

Raymond Loewy's 1953 Studebaker Starliner embodied continental subtlety just as America was peaking in its postwar enthusiasm for automotive behemoths. With its wraparound rear window and clean lines, the Starliner was the first American car to be exhibited in the Museum of Modern Art. Although Loewy's spare design was out of step with the 1950s market, his foresight stood out when the automotive designs of the 1960s picked up on his minimalist cues. Completed in 1961, the theme building at Los Angeles International Airport, designed by a team of architects led by William Pereira, embodied the unbridled dreams and optimism at the dawn of the Jet Age.

This "fantastic" portrait depicts what can only be described as a duel. On the left, the 1959 Cadillac Sedan DeVille. On the right, the 1959 Cadillac Fleetwood 60 Special. To the victor go the spoils, and may the longest tail win.

Winking beneath a chrome eyelid, these twin headlamps belong to the 1959 Dodge
Custom Royal Lancer Convertible.

With its candy-pink paint and swooping tail fins, this 1958 Cadillac Series 62 Coupe DeVille sums up automotive design of the 1950s. Pastel colors and an overabundance of chrome characterized the exuberant cars of the postwar era. All DeVille models were available with cruise control, a two-speaker signal-seeking radio, and an automatic parking-brake release. Ample power was provided, courtesy of a 310-horsepower V-8. Nothing could be finer than cooling off with an evening drive, then topping it off with some ice cream at Mearle's Drive-In in Visalia, California.

It's the late 1950s, and the tail-fin craze is in full swing. Chrysler design stylist Virgil Exner has just designed a number of masterpieces featuring the "Forward Look," a somewhat generic term for his swoopy confections. As a new decade dawned, the big question at Plymouth was, "How do you top perfection?" The answer, of course—you can't. It is not that the 1961 models aren't striking; much of the detailing is actually quite beautiful. But the earlier cars were already extreme, so how much further could Exner go? The resulting automobiles, like this 1961 Plymouth Suburban, embody a bizarre, Rococo quality.

MAY

1 2 3 4 **5** 6 7 8 9 10 11 12 13 14 15 16 17 18 19 20 21 22 23 24 25 26 27 28 29 30 31

Car Lot with Light Bulbs
Visalia, California

MAY

1 2 3 4 5 **6** 7 8 9 10 11 12 13 14 15 16 17 18 19 20 21 22 23 24 25 26 27 28 29 30 31

Considering automobile production numbers worldwide, one has to ask, Where do they all go? This 1987 Breeza, a Ford concept car, is returning to its roots, the sheet-metal junkyard. In the automotive business, sheet metal as well as concepts are frequently recycled.

MAY

What could be more patriotic than a gigantic flag and this true-blue 1967 Chevrolet Corvette Stingray Convertible? Hail to the chief of high performance, Detroit-style.

The E-series represents Mercedes's attempt to update its superb but rather stolid cars into a more youthful mode. This 1999 Mercedes Benz E430 features lighter, more expressive styling than its predecessors. After all, the older generation still has the classic S-class to fall back on.

The 1931 Lincoln Convertible Roadster with a body by Le Baron was extolled for its lovely design.

1937 Studebaker Coupe Express grille

In the early 1930s, Duesenberg supercharged its J models, hence the SJ designation. Only thirty-six SJs were built, including this 1931 Duesenberg Model SJ Torpedo Sedanette with a body by Bohman & Schwartz. Their performance is legendary—104 mph in second gear, topping out at 140 mph. Truly a car for the ages.

MAY

1 2 3 4 5 6 7 8 9 10 11 **12** 13 14 15 16 17 18 19 20 21 22 23 24 25 26 27 28 29 30 31

1911 Pope-Hartford badge

Passengers entered this 1903 Ford Model A at the rear and had their choice of sitting forward or sideward.

Considered by many to be the first mass-produced automobile, the Curved Dash Oldsmobile was first produced in 1902. This 1904 Runabout model is similar in the essential identifying elements: a curved dash and tiller-type steering wheel. Sadly, Oldsmobile is no more.

This stately 1929 Pierce Arrow Model 133 Convertible Coupe featured a rumble seat for the daring (or desperate) passenger.

Many argue the Auburn Automobile Company died because of a marketing miscalculation: the cars were priced too cheaply for the sophisticated enthusiast. Any esteem associated with this marvelously engineered and designed automobile was dashed by its relatively modest sticker price. Today, this powerful and debonair 1932 Auburn Cabriolet conjures up the ultimate marketing dream: an affordable, high-performance luxury car.

In the early days, motoring could be a risky proposition, making a drive of any duration a matter of faith. Consequently, early service stations were often designed like temples to impart trust in their service, just as banks use classical architecture to convey confidence in the financial system. Earl Eckel copied this dramatic 1922 Greek Revival design for Guy's Filling Station in Washington, New Jersey, from a station in Florida. Equally reflective of motoring's stalwart spirit in the early days are the upright lines of this 1927 Willys-Knight Great Six Varsity Roadster. Resulting from the collaboration between the Willys-Overland Company and engineer Charles Knight, the Willys-Knight featured the so-called Silent Knight engine. Only three Varsity Roadsters are known to have survived, perhaps because not every community had a service station of Guy's caliber.

MAY

1 2 3 4 5 6 7 8 9 10 11 12 13 14 15 16 17 **18** 19 20 21 22 23 24 25 26 27 28 29 30 31

Stuckey's
New Mexico

MAY

Big savings! A glut of gasoline in the 1920s forced the price from 25 cents a gallon down to 18 cents a gallon throughout the decade. Good news for the burgeoning motoring public. Automobile ownership tripled in the 1920s.

After World War II, America's industries began retooling for civilian production. One of the first fruits of this industrial transformation was this all-new 1948 Studebaker Commander Coupe. Surrounded by its own "retooling" equipment and automotive paraphernalia, this is a machine in its element. As memorable as the car is the garage that houses it— a male bastion reflecting the mechanical skills and collecting habits of its owner. The Commander's styling is still fresh, displaying the dynamic influence of famed designers Raymond Loewy, Virgil Exner, and their then-young apprentice, Robert E. Bourke. Exner would later go on to design the Chrysler masterpieces of the 1950s.

The initiator of the "pony car revolution," this 1964 ½ Ford Mustang is one of the most influential automotive designs Detroit ever produced. The immediate popularity of these so-called pony cars bolstered Detroit's confidence in producing a line of increasingly faster vehicles, later dubbed "muscle cars." Also representing the best of an era is Billy's Service Station, formerly of Anaheim, California. Sadly, Billy's has fallen victim to the wrecking ball. Sole proprietorships like Billy's fight an uphill battle in an increasingly franchise-driven world.

America's twist on "redhead" (as in Ferrari Testarossa), the 1992 Dodge Viper RT/10's
400-horsepower V-10 engine delivers blistering performance.

MAY

1 2 3 4 5 6 7 8 9 10 11 12 13 14 15 16 17 18 19 20 21 22 **23** 24 25 26 27 28 29 30 31

Perhaps the world's fastest-looking car, this limited-production 1969 Dodge Charger Daytona Hemi sports an enormous wing.

MAY

1 2 3 4 5 6 7 8 9 10 11 12 13 14 15 16 17 18 19 20 21 22 23 **24** 25 26 27 28 29 30 31

The 1963 Chevrolet Corvette Grand Sport, made in extremely limited production, was designed to go head-to-head with the Ford-powered Cobra on the racing circuit. GM's publicly announced policy to not support racing led to an early retirement of these "grandly" conceived racing machines.

Inspired by the original Shelby Cobra, the 1992 Dodge Viper RT/10 is a car designed to evoke memories of the 1960s roadster but with the technology and refinement of a 1990s supercar. Power is provided by a 400-horsepower, aluminum V-10 engine, which, when mated to the six-speed transmission, powers the Viper from 0 to 60 in four seconds. As a prestige publicity vehicle, the Viper's arrival helped pack Dodge's showroom floors during the company's early 1990s turnaround campaign.

For the SUV devotee who wants a bit of European refinement, the 1995 Land Rover Defender fits the bill. For more than half a century, Land Rover has been the vehicle of choice for the "go anywhere, do anything" driver. For urban Americans abandoning cars for SUVs, Land Rover offers more luxury and sophistication than other four-wheeling choices.

MAY

1 2 3 4 5 6 7 8 9 10 11 12 13 14 15 16 17 18 19 20 21 22 23 24 25 26 **27** 28 29 30 31

Rather like Andy Warhol's famous soup can, the 1998 New Beetle is Volkswagen's audacious Pop-art interpretation of the old Beetle. But the mechanics are strictly state of the art, with running gear borrowed from the popular Golf and handling to match.

Packard's merger with Studebaker in the mid-1950s (actually it was a Packard buyout) was a disaster for all concerned. Studebaker had massive production problems and ended up dragging down its relatively healthy parent. A succession of management changes ensued, and soon all Packards were essentially Studebakers with extra chrome. The public wasn't fooled (wags called them "Packardbakers"), and by 1957 only 869 Packard Clipper Country Sedans were produced.

1957 Chevrolet Bel Air Sport Coupe interior

MAY

1 2 3 4 5 6 7 8 9 10 11 12 13 14 15 16 17 18 19 20 21 22 23 24 25 26 27 28 29 **30** 31

1957 Buick Special Coupe dashboard

The Nash Metropolitan, produced from 1954 to 1962, was ahead of its time in demonstrating the virtues of the economy car. Its tiny body was powered by a 1,500-cubic-centimeter, four-cylinder engine with many English-produced parts. American Motors Corporation advertised it as a "go to the market" car, but we prefer the "go to the diner" variation.

Rosie's Diner on Highway M-57 in Rockford, Michigan, is renowned for its great food, homemade pies, and glorious neon: "Good food served right." Manufactured by the Paramount Dining Company in 1945, Rosie's was featured in numerous Bounty Paper Towel commercials where Rosie the waitress wiped counters and declared Bounty to be the "quicker picker-upper" for rapt TV audiences. Patrons of the home cookin' are the occupants of a 1960 Chevrolet Corvette, a 1956 Ford Fairlane Victoria, a 1953 Oldsmobile Rocket 98, a 1960 Cadillac Sedan DeVille, and a 1960 Ford Thunderbird.

JUNE

1 **2** 3 4 5 6 7 8 9 10 11 12 13 14 15 16 17 18 19 20 21 22 23 24 25 26 27 28 29 30

1964 Ford Galaxie 500 Convertible

"We tore a big hole in your convertible top.

What will you tell your Mom and Pop?"

FROM FRANK ZAPPA'S SONG "YOU'RE PROBABLY WONDERING WHY I'M HERE," *MOTHERMANIA*, 1969

As with sports cars and showboat vehicles, the pickup truck is another 1950s automotive genre that scored a powerful comeback in the 1990s. Some things never change, and the American desire to haul cargo is one of them. The Johnny Rockets chain of classic diners also stays true to its heritage, offering an unaltered 1950s tradition of burgers, dogs, and fries around the clock.

Sunset is an appropriate setting for this 1951 Mercury Station Wagon, which is one of the last actual woody wagons—cars with real wood sides instead of the fake paneling that appeared in the early 1960s.

1948 Ford Woody Wagon

The boxy shape and warm woodwork of this 1929 Ford Model A Station Wagon make it look a little like a garden shed on wheels. Many of these workhorse Ford station wagons were used as farm vehicles.

"In 1936, our family of five left Milford, Nebraska. We had a 1929 Model A Ford and an 18-foot trailer/mobile home that a neighbor and I had built. . . . We had eaten everything edible, so we gave ourselves a treat and ate at the local café [in Amarillo]. Meals were $.35 each, and coffee was $.90 to fill the jug. The local store had no snacks, but the owner did give us a bag of dried apples for a dollar. . . .

[The road to Albuquerque] was the worst of all the roads, complete with mountains that went straight up and then straight down. On one, before getting to Albuquerque, we almost didn't get to the top. Low gear and slipping the tired clutch put us over. Then at a curve on the downside (we were going 35 mph in low), there was a group of bandits stretched across the road to stop us, but our screaming engine scared them away.

At the California line we got our sticker and 'Welcome to California' brochure. We were just more 'Okies,' and there were many of us. Wow! We had arrived. After making it over the final pass, we started to see orange groves. All you could drink for $.10! Thompson grapes for $.10 a peck! Love this place!"

JAY BANNISTER, ROSAMOND, CALIFORNIA

The death of Route 66, the birth of Interstate 40. From Goldroad, Arizona:

"This was once a major road between Los Angeles and Chicago, and I can't imagine the goods of commerce passing this way. How time has changed the events of the past decades, and yet what is truly important has stayed the same. The quiet isolation, the clean, clear sky at night that revealed every constellation, the faces of the Native Americans, which told a story without speaking a word."

GERARD SMITH, TALLAHASSEE, FLORIDA

Kaveneys Pharmacy, with its bright red ceramic facade, was the centerpiece of town in the days when tiny Wilmington, Illinois, was struggling to establish itself. Times changed with the suburban migration, but Kaveneys was saved by owners who turned it into an antiques emporium. Tough times also led to the memorable design of the 1931 Chrysler Sport Roadster. Contending with the Depression, Chrysler had to create the most seductive car possible. Designers took inspiration from the Cord L-29 luxury sedan and scored big with this roadster's racy, low-slung styling and a straight-eight engine. Like Kaveneys, this roadster has survived because its classic original design earned the care and attention of preservation-minded owners.

Like thoroughbreds at a trough, these stunning finned fifties mobiles line up at famed Mearle's Drive-In of Visalia, California. In the 1940s and 1950s, Mearle's was a renowned destination for those seeking to beat the Central California heat. Carhop service allowed sweltering patrons to enjoy ice cream or a soda without having to leave the car. The advent of air-conditioning in 1963 changed the habits of Mearle's patrons, who then preferred indoor dining. Nevertheless, curbside service remains an option since Mearle's is faithful to its history.

JUNE

1 2 3 4 5 6 7 8 9 **10** 11 12 13 14 15 16 17 18 19 20 21 22 23 24 25 26 27 28 29 30

1935 Brewster Convertible

The Packard motto was "Ask the Man Who Owns One," relying on word of mouth to spread the company's reputation for quality. Packard's celebrated Ray Dietrich designed the impressive body of this 1933 Packard V-12 Sport Phaeton.

Wild tales of murder, mayhem, tortured Indian spirits, and buried treasure continue to haunt Two Guns, Arizona, located between Flagstaff and Winslow. Once Route 66 was certified, these myths were powerful enough to prompt the opening of a genuine tourist trap at Two Guns—featuring a wild animal zoo, a curio shop, and a gas station—which later burned down in a mysterious fire. A straight-8 Ford engine powers this 1935 Ford Pickup, which stands in front of the long-gone "Mountain Lions" cage of Two Gun's wild animal zoo. This 1935 Ford ½-ton pickup dates from the era when Henry Ford's reign over the American automobile market was on the wane. Chrysler and GM were nipping at the aging Ford's heels, but the introduction of the V-8 engine gave Ford a burst of speed that lasted to the end of World War II.

"Outside of Holbrook, Arizona, I helped a woman change a tire. When I was finished, she went to the back of her pickup and cut me a piece of homemade apple pie. I told her I'd follow her into Holbrook, and as I drove by, she waved to me and I could read her lips saying thanks a lot."

HERBERT REITKER, SR., LA MIRADA, CALIFORNIA

The front end of this 1939 Chrysler Imperial Station Wagon suggests a grand touring car while the wood paneling of the rear gives the car a friendly, approachable look. This car is just right for a family interested in seeing the world in style.

From the mid- to late 1940s, Martha Oakes and her siblings made several moves between Indiana and Arizona with her dad, who drove a truck, and her mom, who drove the family Packard:

"As we slowly crossed the country on Route 66, I practiced 'speed reading' by never missing a Burma Shave series and learned map-reading skills by tracking our trip with a red crayon on the frayed and aging road map. Mother had taught school, and she never completely put away her lesson book. . . . We didn't nap or tease one another, we were too busy listening to Mother as she drove with one hand and pointed and talked with the other.

. . . We would follow Daddy into a shady glen near a farm. This would be our campsite. Out came the table; little ones were sent to the nearby farm for water, older ones built a campfire, and soon a hot meal was shared on our own familiar table with the tablecloth and wildflowers. After breakfast [the next day], the table was cleared and schoolbooks came out for the day's assignments. Book lessons were completed while we drove, when Mother wasn't teaching from the landscape."

MARTHA M. OAKES, ORANGE PARK, FLORIDA

Woodies

Encinitas, California

The surfer rode to the forefront of popular culture like winged Mercury on a longboard.
The Beach Boys' pop music hit "Surfin' U.S.A." (1963) and campy surfer movies like
Beach Party (1964), starring Annette Funicello and Frankie Avalon, added extra cachet
to a Southern California lifestyle envied the world over.

JUNE

1 2 3 4 5 6 7 8 9 10 11 12 13 14 **15** 16 17 18 19 20 21 22 23 24 25 26 27 28 29 30

The Ford Mustang found new competition when its cousin, the sensationally powerful Shelby GT-350, was introduced. This 1965 model was hard to beat at the stoplight. The GT-350 got its start when Lee Iacocca called upon racing legend Carroll Shelby to create a car that would be capable of defeating the dominant small-block Corvettes on the S.C.C.A. racing circuit.

There may be no more flagrant a speed-demon car ever built than this 1970 Plymouth Superbird. Arriving at the end of Detroit's fuel-squandering era, the Superbird is a street-legal race car that was mass-produced only to meet NASCAR requirements for a production vehicle. Less than 2,000 Superbirds were made and only a few were sold to us mere mortals on the streets. Soaring like an architectural version of the Superbird's spoiler are the golden arches of this McDonald's Restaurant in Downey, California. One of the few original surviving examples of the world-famous burger franchise, this McDonald's has remained intact since 1953. It is a reminder of the days when the golden arches played a structural role as roof supports guaranteed to catch the eyes and appetites of passing motorists.

Storm clouds are brewing on the horizon as a battle looms between red and yellow outside of the Teaneck Dairy Queen in Fort Lee, New Jersey. In red is the famous Yenko Camaro (1969 SE) that was customized by dealer Don Yenko of Pennsylvania with a big-block 427 cid V-8: these engines proved so popular that Chevy began supplying Yenko with the engines preinstalled. Packing its own sting is this bumblebee-yellow Camaro, the quiet middle sibling between big Impala and little Nova. It's secret weapon? The SS (Super-Sport) package that includes a 350+-horsepower V-8. When these babies get going that red roof better be securely bolted to its vanilla moorings.

In 1960, Dodge tried to identify its passenger cars with the dawning of the space age. Thus, a rocket-ship motif can be found throughout the detailing of the Dodge Polara Sport Coupe, shown at Kohr's Frozen Custard in Seaside Heights, New Jersey. Dodge even borrowed the model name from the Polaris missile. Special futuristic features include a push-button transmission and a built-in "satellite" clock that resembles a compass.

JUNE

1 2 3 4 5 6 7 8 9 10 11 12 13 14 15 16 17 18 **19** 20 21 22 23 24 25 26 27 28 29 30

The Santa Rosa, New Mexico, segment of Route 66 offers one of the most romantic two-lane stretches of highway anywhere on earth. Speeding along the empty road, the staccato rhythm of telephone poles is the only reminder of civilization. The shimmering heat, the wide-open vistas, and the chirping crickets cast an almost hypnotic spell on the traveler, especially if you're lucky enough to be driving a vintage automobile with the top down or a 1957 Chevrolet Cameo pickup truck. Sample some of the local Mexican food and head on out to the great beyond.

One of the greatest tourist traps of all time, the Jack Rabbit Trading Post in Joseph City, Arizona, has been luring Route 66 travelers since 1949. Founder Jim Taylor, a marketing whiz, borrowed from the success of early Burma Shave roadside advertisements; he posted a series of small, enigmatic yellow signs featuring a black jackrabbit along with the number of miles left until arrival. The ploy worked—kids clamored to see the rabbit and road-fatigued parents were more than willing to oblige. This original billboard proudly announces your arrival.

In 1949, nine-year-old Floyd Farrar traveled with his grandparents to visit relatives in Albuquerque, New Mexico:

"They had purchased a new '49 Chevy and wanted to get some miles on it to break in the engine. You had to do that in those days. . . . I absolutely loved the Burma Shave signs, I could never get enough of them. Then the signs that all you could see was a black outline of a jackrabbit with a number of miles beneath it. We couldn't understand what it meant. You would find them up on the sides of hills, back in canyons, almost anywhere you'd least expect it. They would always say that you are getting closer to it. Then when we finally arrived it was only a trading post.

I remembered this particular curio shop so vividly by the signs, that on one trip a while back, I endeavored to find it. It is still there alongside old Route 66 near Holbrook, Arizona, near the Petrified Forest."

FLOYD L. FARRAR, HAWAIIAN GARDENS, CALIFORNIA

Although Interstate 40 bypassed Tucumcari, New Mexico, the city has remained vital due in part to an ingenious roadside billboard campaign urging weary motorists onward to "Tucumcari Tonite! 2000 Motel Rooms." Tucumcari today: "Where superhighways now rush, prehistoric man once hunted."

"It took us a full day to travel from Cincinnati to St. Louis, and another from St. Louis to Joplin. Therefore, we always stayed overnight in St. Louis in a motel, which was a big adventure. Grandpa always drove an up-to-date Buick, and we always packed our thermos and lunch for a picnic along the way. It was always my sister's and my responsibility to watch for the sign for a 'Roadside Table.' Sometimes, we'd just pull off the road and set up our own card table to eat [on]. Soon it was time to watch for motel signs. Grandma would immediately ask to 'see the room' so she could check the beds and cleanliness. This is something that was done in the years of the 1940s and early 1950s.

. . . Motels grew larger and added more attractions. But the big excitement came when we began stopping several times before settling on THE motel, asking whether they had a pool. Now when we packed for the trip, we always made sure we packed our dour swimsuits."

BARBARA (WORZ) GODDARD AND NANCY (WORZ) NEFF, CINCINNATI, OHIO

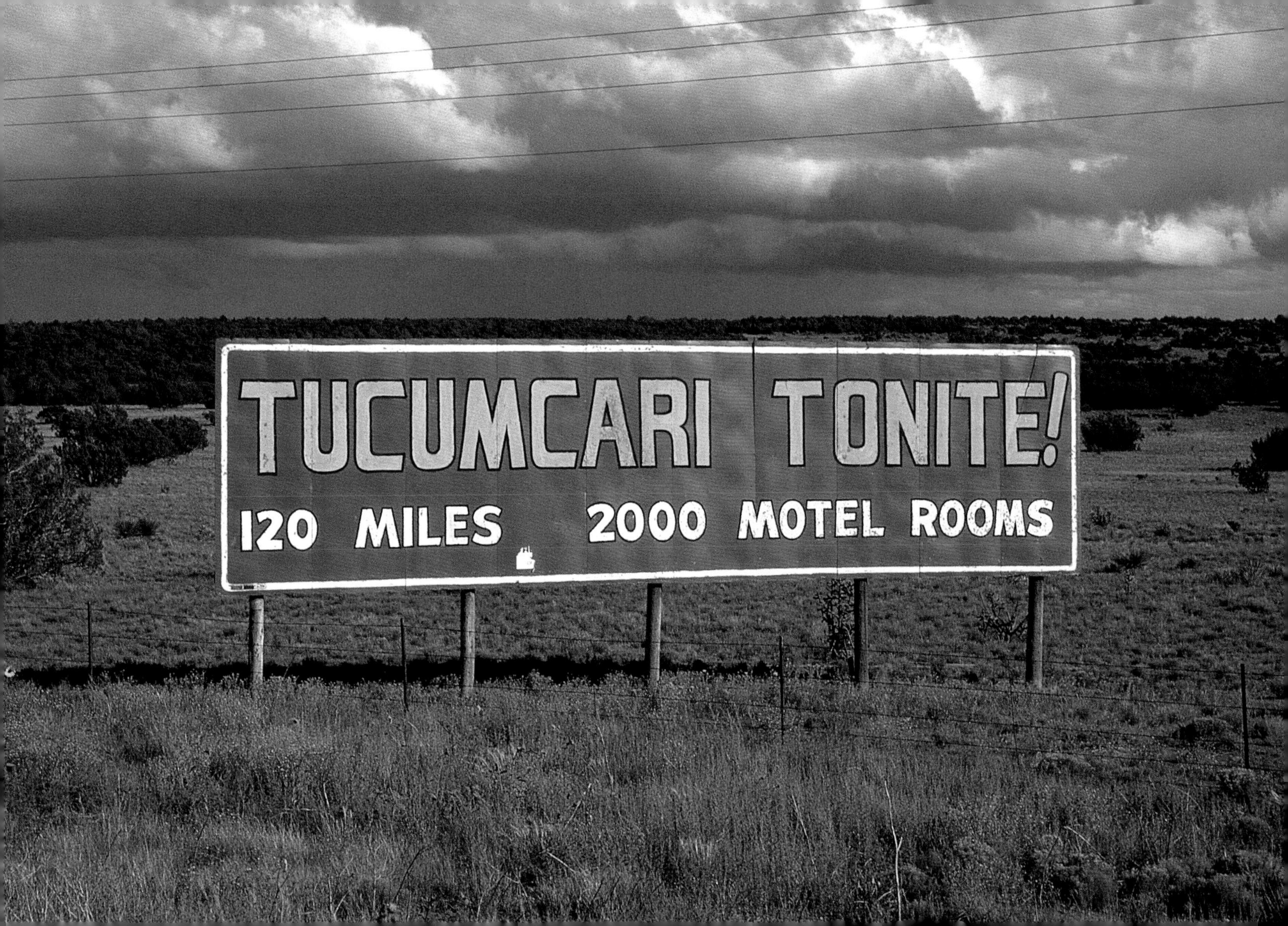
TUCUMCARI TONITE!
120 MILES 2000 MOTEL ROOMS

The 1957 Cameo was Chevrolet's top-of-the-line pickup. Although handsomely styled, what really sets it apart is its smooth-sided fenderless truck bed and wide sunshade mounted over the windshield. An unusual option for this year was this "traffic light viewer," a dash-mounted reflector that allows the driver to see the traffic light above without having to crane his neck under the sunshade. A low-tech answer to a nagging inconvenience.

Chief Yellow Horse Trading Post west of Gallup, New Mexico

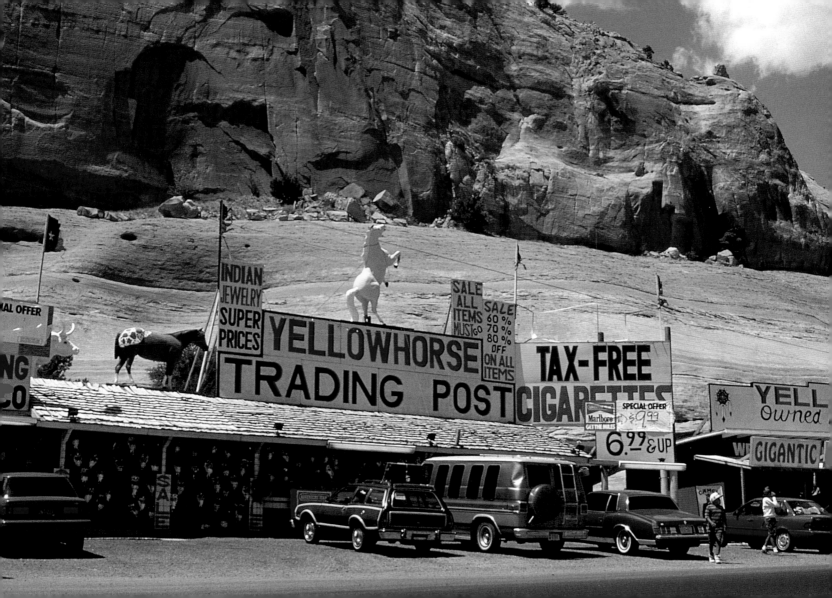

Tourist Trap
New Mexico

Before the postwar highway boom of the 1950s, the intrepid traveler along Route 66 might haul his own tent and cook gear in this stylish 1947 Chevrolet Stylemaster with matching luggage rack.

"Being of Afro-American heritage, I recall specifically the lack of accommodations for lodging and dining for the (then) 'Colored.' Two outstanding incidents are etched in my memory— one in Flagstaff, Arizona, and another in a town in Texas. Realizing the discrimination of the day, I sought out a Mexican restaurant (off the route) in which to feed myself and family in Flagstaff. Much to my surprise, we were refused service—and this was not the case in Los Angeles! [In a small town in Texas], I had grown weary from driving and sought out a Police Station for information on the location of a 'Colored' motel. If anyone had reliable information on a safe place to lodge overnight, the police certainly would be a good source, was my reasoning. The officer informed me 'there was none,' but made a kind offer of the use of an open cell! Of course, we declined the offer!"

ED ALLEN, VICTORVILLE, CALIFORNIA

JUNE

1 2 3 4 5 6 7 8 9 10 11 12 13 14 15 16 17 18 19 20 21 22 23 24 25 **26** 27 28 29 30

This Phillips 66 station has been faithfully preserved by the locals of McLean, Texas. McLean has another "must-see" Route 66 attraction: the Devil's Rope Museum. Anyone interested in the Wild West or Route 66 will enjoy the astounding collection of barbwire fencing known as Devil's Rope as well as an extensive oral history by many 66 old-timers from the Texas Panhandle.

A pristine example of the Victorian-style structures built to serve American railroads in their heyday, this depot is located in Galena, Kansas. These days the depot functions as a Mining and Historical Museum, commemorating the days when Galena was a mining boomtown for lead and zinc. During the boom Galena was served by no less than three separate railroad lines. Ironically, the 1931 Model A Ford helped replace the railroads as America's primary form of public transportation: Americans preferred the flexibility of driving to the schedules of trains. So eagerly awaited was the Model A (the successor to Ford's top-selling Model T) that police were called out on its arrival to restrain curious crowds in a number of cities. With a reasonable $475 price tag and four cylinders pumping 40 horsepower, the Model A helped Ford stay on top of the market.

J. Nagy Jr. of South Bend, Indiana, collected this beautiful 1928 Route 66 map. He picked it up while hitchhiking from South Bend to Los Angeles in 1930. He first traveled Lincoln Highway, then picked up Route 66 into California. Sleeping under the stars on old newspapers, he completed the trip in ten days.

PACIFIC TIME WEST OF SALTLAKE CITY

OGDEN. 38
PROVO 42
THISTLE
CASTLEGATE
PRICE 12
66
ELGIN 28
MOAB JCT. 24
MOAB
67
MONTICELLO 79

WHITE CAFE GALLUP N.M.

MESA VERDE N.P.
AZTEC RUIN
DOLORES 12
CORTEZ 16
MANCOS 30
DURANGO
SOUTH FORK
SHIPROCK 32
FARMINGTON
TOCITO 25
DROLET
CHACO CANYON NAT'L MONUMENT
41
GAMERCO
SEVEN LAKES
THOREAU
BACA
BLUEWATER
GRANTS
LAGUNA
ICE CAVES
SAN FIDEL
ACOMA
SUWANEE
RIO PUERCO
LOS LUNAS
ISLETA

GALLUP
HOUCK
LUPTON
CHAMBERS 22
NAVAJO
EL MORRO 11
RAMAH 22

MESA BRIDGE 11
KAYENTA
A CITY
ORAIBI
CAFF TOREVA
NONA POLACCA
KEAMS CANYON

REST ROOM

COMPLIMENTS OF
WHITE CAFE
THE PLACE
TO EAT

OPEN DAY & NIGHT

SLOW
HOLBROOK
PETRIFIED FORES
STATE INSPECTION DEPOT WESTWARD
PAINTED DESERT

MILEAGE DIAGRAM FROM LOS ANGELES TO DENVER

LOS ANGELES 1870
DENVER
PUEBLO
WALSENBURG
TRINIDAD
SANTA FE
ALBUQUERQUE
GALLUP
FLAGSTAFF
WINSLOW
NEEDLES
BARSTOW

CHEYENNE
PIERCE
PLATTEVILLE
FT. LUPTON
DOVER
GREELEY
GILCREST
BRIGHTON
DENVER
LITTLETON
SEDALIA
CASTLEROCK
LARKSPUR
MONUMENT
PIKEVIEW
COLORADO SPRS
FOUNTAIN
BUTTES
PINON
PUEBLO
ABBEY
CROW
GREENHORN
APACHE
WALSENBURG
LA VETA
AGUILAR
CHICOSA
EARL
EL MORRO
TRINIDAD
GALLINAS
RATON
MAXWELL
FRENCH
SPRINGER
COLMAR
NOLAN
WAGON MOUND
SHOEMAKER
WATROUS
ONAVA
LAS VEGAS
SANTA ROSA
NEWKIRK

DELNORTE
MONTEVISTA 14
ALAMOSA 17
60
WOLF CR. PASS
PAGOSA SPRS
PIEDRA
DULCE
RIVERSIDE
AZTEC
CIMARRON
TAOS 54 26
ESPANOLA 50
POJUAQUE 19
SANTA FE
LA BAJADA
BERNALILLO
GLORIETTA
PECOS
ROMEROVILLE
MORIARITI
ALBUQUERQUE

NEW MEXICO

KANSAS
MOUNTAIN TIME WEST OF
CENTER OF U.S.

ROCKYFORD
LA JUNTA
FOWLER
VINELAND
BLOOM
TIMPAS
LOS ANIMAS
HASTY
GRANADA
LAMAR
COOLIDGE
SYRACUSE
KENDALL
DEERFIELD
LAKIN
GARDEN CITY
CHARLESTON
DODGE CITY
CIMARRON CITY
LINDSBO
LYONS
GREAT BENT
ELLINWOOD
LARNED
RAFFORD
OFFERLE
GREAT BENT
SAL

TEXAS
OKLA.
AMARILLO
U.S. 66
GLENRIO
ENDEE
VEGA
WILDORAD
CONWAY
GROOM
JERICHO
McLEAN
SHAMROCK
TEXOLA
ERICK
SAYRE
ELK CITY
WEATHERFORD
BRIDGEPORT
GEARY

Early advertisers exploited the commercial potential of the open road by paying farmers to allow signs to be painted on their barns. Parked in front is a 1929 Chevrolet Phaeton featuring a "Stovebolt Six" engine, so named for its utilitarian slotted head bolts. This engine configuration gave Chevrolet an extra two cylinders over its four-cylinder Ford rival, and by 1927 Chevys were outselling Fords.

Every weekend, rain or shine, summer and winter, Helen Tobias Martin and her family traveled from St. Louis to Sullivan, Missouri:

"My first trip on 66 was in 1929 in a touring car with side curtains. A few times, I remember starting out in the morning and not arriving till late afternoon—a matter of about 80 miles. Sometimes I sat between Dad and Uncle Joe. Dad played the harmonica, we all sang, and the men always had a crock with 'home brew.' We always stopped at the Diamonds for gas and popcorn coming and going.

We would pull over just outside of St. Clair city limits. We would split open a watermelon and eat under the shade of this big oak tree—no speeding cars—no nothing."

HELEN TOBIAS MARTIN, SULLIVAN, MISSOURI

JUNE

1 2 3 4 5 6 7 8 9 10 11 12 13 14 15 16 17 18 19 20 21 22 23 24 25 26 27 28 29 **30**

1928 Packard Convertible Coupe wheel

JULY

1 2 3 4 5 6 7 8 9 10 11 12 13 14 15 16 17 18 19 20 21 22 23 24 25 26 27 28 29 30 31

1919 Ballot Indianapolis Race Car. With the end of World War I and a need to promote new markets for its engines, French manufacturer Ballot decided to pursue automobile racing. The tactic had proven successful for Henry Ford in the early 1900s, and Ballot saw the postwar resurrection of the Indianapolis 500 as an opportunity to build this racer for some needed publicity.

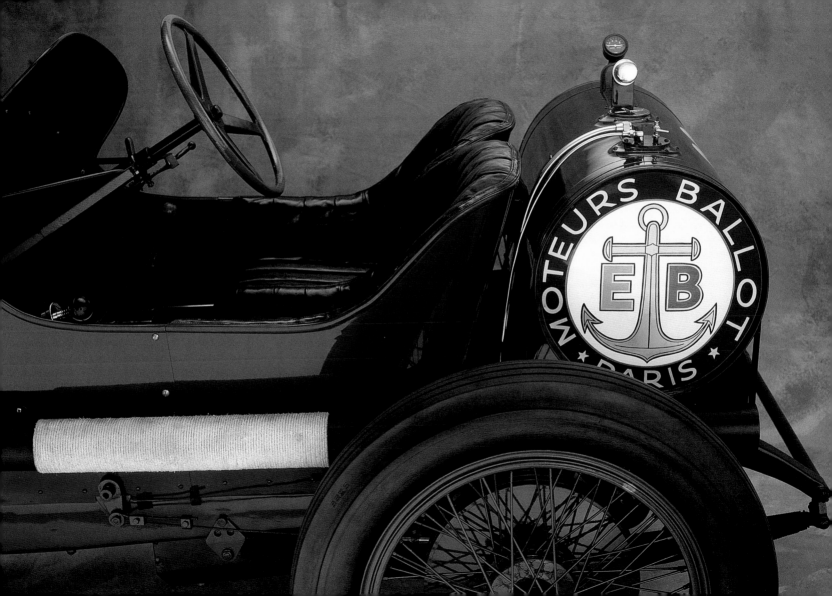

JULY

1 **2** 3 4 5 6 7 8 9 10 11 12 13 14 15 16 17 18 19 20 21 22 23 24 25 26 27 28 29 30 31

With its round beveled windshield and snazzy brass trim, this 1910 Marion Special
Roadster declares its complete independence from the horse-and-buggy era. It represents
a new style—a style shaped by speed.

JULY

1 2 3 4 5 6 7 8 9 10 11 12 13 14 15 16 17 18 19 20 21 22 23 24 25 26 27 28 29 30 31

1900 Packard Runabout wheel

What could be more American than this 1957 Ford Thunderbird? Ford did not create the Thunderbird just because of competition from the hot new two-seater Corvette; it had other good reasons as well. GIs returning from World War II coveted the svelte European sports cars they saw while stationed overseas and were ready to hit the road in America's counterparts.

JULY

1 2 3 4 5 6 7 8 9 10 11 12 13 14 15 16 17 18 19 20 21 22 23 24 25 26 27 28 29 30 31

Grand Canyon Rail Stop

Williams, Arizona

JULY

1 2 3 4 5 6 7 8 9 10 11 12 13 14 15 16 17 18 19 20 21 22 23 24 25 26 27 28 29 30 31

Ed's Camp

Mojave Desert, Arizona

JULY

1 2 3 4 5 6 7 8 9 10 11 12 13 14 15 16 17 18 19 20 21 22 23 24 25 26 27 28 29 30 31

Desert Hot Rod
Kingman, Arizona

The plan for a transcontinental highway—Route 66—was announced in 1926, and the famed road attracted coast-to-coast travelers well before its completion in the mid-1930s. Many segments of the road remained unimproved for years, veering from pavement to gravel to dirt that became deeply rutted by the heavy traffic. As a result, traveling Route 66 in the early days was an ordeal not far removed from the struggles of the pioneer wagon trains that preceded the automobile in journeys westward. Early Route 66 travelers often had the same sense of manifest destiny that drove their pioneer forebears, leading to the highway's early nickname, "the Mother Road." Automotive design was still at a preliminary stage, so driving was truly an adventure.

JULY

1 2 3 4 5 6 7 8 9 10 11 12 13 14 15 16 17 18 19 20 21 22 23 24 25 26 27 28 29 30 31

More than any other SUV, the Grand Cherokee is responsible for stoking the sport-utility craze of the 1990s. Originally designed as an off-road vehicle, the Grand Cherokee has become extremely popular with urban and suburban drivers wanting to convey a rough-and-ready image. The Grand Cherokee pictured here is off-road, far from domestication of any kind. Highly unusual.

After flooding the American market with economy cars in the late 1970s and 1980s, the Japanese bested the Germans in the 1990s luxury-car market via the Lexus. This 1992 Lexus SC-400 is emblematic of Japan's inroads. The key advantage of the Lexus was its incredible reliability, which the more persnickety German cars had never matched despite high levels of luxury and craftsmanship.

JULY

1 2 3 4 5 6 7 8 9 10 **11** 12 13 14 15 16 17 18 19 20 21 22 23 24 25 26 27 28 29 30 31

Looking like a vehicle from Neptune, this Pontiac Protosport concept car features a host of stylistic innovations from the past and future. The gull-wing doors and tungsten headlights make this car truly a post–space-age vehicle. It is a design approach that opens a whole new world of possibilities.

JULY

1 2 3 4 5 6 7 8 9 10 11 **12** 13 14 15 16 17 18 19 20 21 22 23 24 25 26 27 28 29 30 31

Check out the squared-off, transparent Lucite steering wheel in this 1961 Plymouth Suburban—an automotive first (and, as far as we know, last). And how about that "twin pod" instrumentation?

1 2 3 4 5 6 7 8 9 10 11 12 **13** 14 15 16 17 18 19 20 21 22 23 24 25 26 27 28 29 30 31

The GTO is considered Detroit's first true "muscle car," and with its optional 389 "Tri-Power" V-8 (translation: a 360-horsepower, *three-carburetor* engine), it's not hard to see why. Basically a performance spin-off of the Tempest, the 1965 Pontiac GTO took the American motoring public by storm. Options included a floor shift, quick steering, a four-speed gearbox, metallic brake linings, and a "posi-traction rear end" (a limited slip differential). This transformed the modest but solid Tempest into one of the greatest high-performance bargains of all time.

JULY

1 2 3 4 5 6 7 8 9 10 11 12 13 **14** 15 16 17 18 19 20 21 22 23 24 25 26 27 28 29 30 31

A two-tone palette of pastel colors was a popular paint choice in the 1950s. This 1955
Plymouth Belvedere in peach and cream flaunted a head-turning combination.

Before the days of air-conditioning, drivers sweltering through the Arizona desert dreamed of staying cool. Motels like the Starlite erected neon artwork to exploit those fantasies, aiming to bring even the most callous speed demon to a grinding halt. Like a Siren to the sweaty traveler, the bathing-suited lady dives in an endlessly repeating cascade of neon, leaving us to imagine the splash as she plunges into the motel's frosty-cool swimming pool. For jousting matches on the American road, a knight-errant could have no better steed than this Dodge Custom Royal Lancer convertible. The Medieval heraldry of armor, lance, and shield conceal a nearly space-age level of comfort and technical innovation.

JULY

1 2 3 4 5 6 7 8 9 10 11 12 13 14 15 **16** 17 18 19 20 21 22 23 24 25 26 27 28 29 30 31

This Sinclair station in Odell, Illinois, recalls the vanished prefranchise era, when gas stations offered more than just gas. In those days, the magic words "fill 'er up" launched a battalion of attendants into action: they would check the oil and clean the windshield as a matter of course and were ready with knowledgeable advice on a host of mechanical questions. Similarly, this 1946 Chrysler Royal recalls a more genteel era—its optional sun visor greets the viewer as if tipping its hat.

JULY

1 2 3 4 5 6 7 8 9 10 11 12 13 14 15 16 **17** 18 19 20 21 22 23 24 25 26 27 28 29 30 31

Packard offered air-conditioning—called Packard Weather Conditioning—for the
first time in its 1940 models, including this Packard 110 Convertible. Air-conditioning
remained a prized luxury option until the 1960s. One can only imagine how prized it might
have been to the occupants of this car while traveling in the desert heat that encircles
this Arizona trading post.

The V-16 engine, introduced in 1930, is what sets this 1931 Cadillac Fleetwood Phaeton apart from its prestigious competition. The overhead-valve engine provided exceptional acceleration with minimal shifting, making this car truly fleet of feet.

JULY

1   2   3   4   5   6   7   8   9   10   11   12   13   14   15   16   17   18   **19**   20   21   22   23   24   25   26   27   28   29   30   31

The 1997 XK8 was Jaguar's first all-new model since the XJS of the early 1970s. The Jaguar faithful were alarmed that Ford's corporate takeover would mean the end of this marque's unique character. Fortunately, Ford added a needed boost of reliability but preserved the classic Jaguar aura.

This 1955 Chevrolet Bel Air top-of-the-line convertible was a high-class ride that featured Chevrolet's first V-8 engine. There is a suggestion of a jet-age aesthetic, but the car retains an organic friendliness, with visored headlights giving it an almost animal demeanor. One of the friendliest restaurants ever is Bob's Big Boy, a fast-food franchise whose mascot is the smiling big boy with a huge burger held aloft. This branch is the oldest surviving example of the chain. Designed in 1949 by architect Wayne McAllister, it epitomizes postwar "Coffee Shop Moderne" architecture and was recently declared a historic landmark in its hometown of Burbank, California.

If manna is from heaven, what is the origin of this white 1959 Oldsmobile Super 88 Holiday Scenicoup? Detroit cooked up a masterwork with this land yacht, a term that is no exaggeration: it's a full nine inches wider and ten inches longer than any previous model. It's even bigger than the White Manna! The Art Deco–inspired White Manna Hamburger Diner was actually built for the 1939 World's Fair to give visitors a futuristic look at fast food. Manna burgers are quite small—about the size of a flattened golf ball. This Olds could eat more than a few.

Like the opening chords of a song by Led Zeppelin or Aerosmith, the 1970 Plymouth Superbird cannot fail to be noticed wherever its rubber hits the road. This baby runs as fast as it looks. It was designed as a race car and mass-produced solely to qualify it as a production car under NASCAR rules. When NASCAR increased the production run required to qualify, Plymouth obliged by making another 1,400 birds. The Superbird's star turn occurred in the 1970 Daytona 500, where it beat out every Ford and Dodge competitor. Alas, the Superbird became extinct when NASCAR changed the rules again the following year. This particular bird lives on, however, nurtured by Mike Venardi of Simi Valley, California.

Beef Burger
Amarillo, Texas

In 1949 the American Dream was gradually rising from the ashes of World War II, with
its memories of shortage and hardship. This 1949 Ford Deluxe Business Coupe reflects
a dream that's still hesitant. With its low ratio of window space to body mass, the Ford
seems tanklike. Later designs had the confidence to open up the proportion of glass
and create panoramic visibility. Hinting at the prosperity on the horizon, this model was
specifically tailored to salesmen, with the back seat omitted to allow for their sample
cases as they traveled from city to city. The rich oxblood color and robust form of this car
give it a visual if not a thematic fellowship with the bovine mascot of the unforgettable
Beef Burger restaurant in Amarillo, Texas.

The 1965 Pontiac GTO could be the dictionary definition of a hot rod. Also red hot is Rod's Steak House of Williams, Arizona. It was founded in 1946 by Rod Graves, a surveyor, who served steaks from his Hereford cattle ranch. As with many Route 66 institutions, Rod's was sold by its founder to longtime employees who continue to maintain its superlative standards.

Rod's STEAK HOUSE
COCKTAILS & DINING
Rod's STEAK HOUSE
SLAGEL ST
E. RAILROAD AVE
OPEN
COCKTAILS & DINING
ENTRANCE
ENTRANCE
Est. 1946
Historic Business
ROUTE 66
Rod's STEAK HOUSE
G.T.O.
HOOSIER
RADIAL GT

The 1956 Ford Thunderbird

JULY

1 2 3 4 5 6 7 8 9 10 11 12 13 14 15 16 17 18 19 20 21 22 23 24 25 **26** 27 28 29 30 31

Life certainly would be "nice" behind the wheel of this 1961 Buick Invicta, either with or without the Coca-Cola.

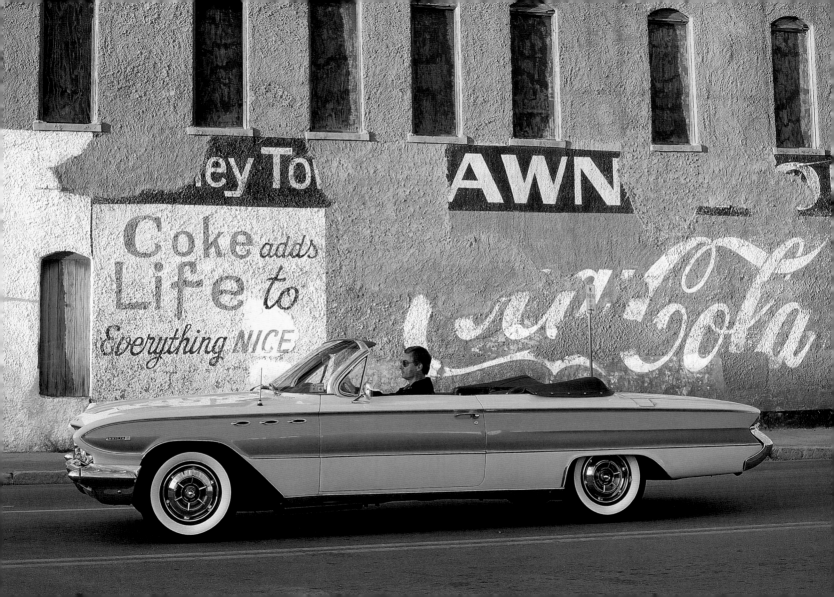

JULY

1 2 3 4 5 6 7 8 9 10 11 12 13 14 15 16 17 18 19 20 21 22 23 24 25 26 **27** 28 29 30 31

Like a refugee from a cartoon world, this 1959 Studebaker Lark motors down Route 66 on a prototypical Main Street in Stroud, Oklahoma. The Lark's clean, unassuming lines proved a big hit when the car was introduced in 1959, tipping off automotive designers that the public had had enough of the chrome mania and designer excesses of the late 1950s.

DRINK
Coca-Cola
Coca-Cola
Sweets-N-Eats
OPEN
WELCOME
STROUD, OK.

Geography purists might carp that Coney Island is far removed from this restaurant in the landlocked Massachusetts city of Worcester. But hey, is every Paris cleaners in Paris? Worcester's Coney Island hot dogs—originally cut from a spool by the jolly proprietor— are famous and are every bit as juicy as their New York progenitors. Under the enormous enamel-and-neon sign of a hot dog dripping mustard sits another classic: the 1957 Chevrolet Bel Air.

JULY

1 2 3 4 5 6 7 8 9 10 11 12 13 14 15 16 17 18 19 20 21 22 23 24 25 26 27 28 **29** 30 31

The corrugated metal roof of this carnival ride is a perfect foil for the aerodynamic edge of this 1966 Chevrolet Corvette 427 Convertible. The Corvette's gills accentuate its sharklike demeanor: this baby is hungry for chum.

The eccentric Space Age Lodge in Gila Bend, Arizona, and this supercool 1960 Cadillac Fleetwood Model 60 Special Four-Door Sedan both reflect the same 1960s phenomenon— the mystical lure of outer space and America's obsession to get there.

JULY

1 2 3 4 5 6 7 8 9 10 11 12 13 14 15 16 17 18 19 20 21 22 23 24 25 26 27 28 29 30 **31**

1968 Chevrolet Chevelle SS 396

Gleaming like faceted baubles showcased in a jeweler's window, these fine gauges are mounted in the enameled dashboard of a 1929 Duesenberg Model J Dual Cowl Phaeton.

This fanciful prototype, a 1948 Tasco Sport Coupe, has an interior clearly inspired by aviation cockpits.

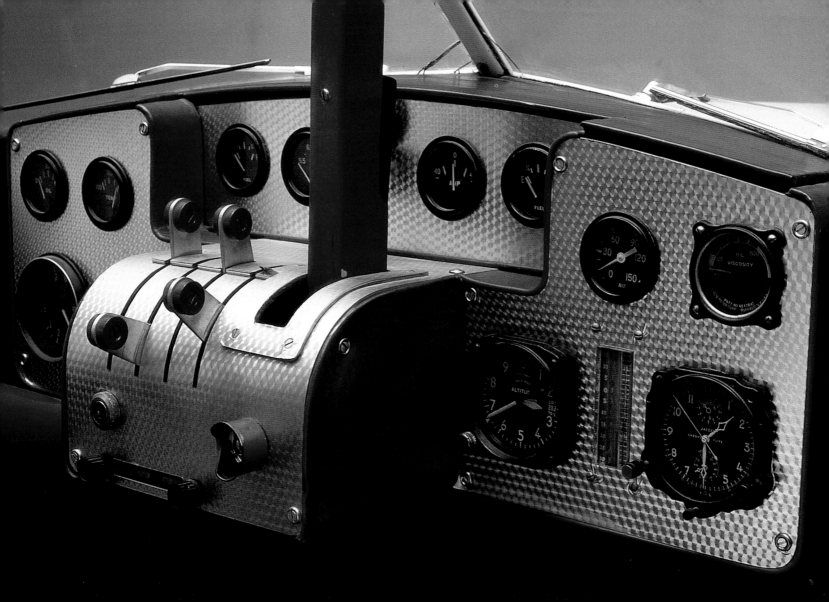

The toothy grille of this 1948 Buick Roadmaster presents a blinding array of chrome, earning it the moniker "The Million Dollar Grin." It is a little like your fat-cat Uncle Marvin showing off his expensive new bridgework at a family gathering.

AUGUST

1 2 3 **4** 5 6 7 8 9 10 11 12 13 14 15 16 17 18 19 20 21 22 23 24 25 26 27 28 29 30 31

Let's cruise the drive-in on a hot summer night in a 1962 Chevrolet Biscayne.

In 1946, the gigantic "66" Park In Theatre in St. Louis, Missouri, opened for business on Route 66. At the time, it boasted the largest drive-in screen in the city, a distinction it held until its demise in 1994. The drive-in theater was devised in the era before air-conditioning to provide entertainment on a hot summer's night while the house cooled down. It was an activity for the whole family, with a twilight show and a playground designed to exhaust the youngsters so more mature folks could enjoy the movie.

1940 Packard Custom Station Wagon

1930 DuPont Royal Town Car

The 1937 Cord Model 812 Berline Limousine was built for speed, and this glorious strip of two-lane blacktop is just the place to see how fast she'll go.

The telephone poles along this flat stretch of road in California's Central Valley roll by in endless procession. Residents in such country often opt for transportation that contrasts with the landscape, as is certainly the case with this revamped red-hot 1934 Ford Coupe.

Boyd Coddington transformed this 1933 Ford into a modern-day hot rod. Inspired by the souped-up cars of the 1950s, Coddington caters to the men who have made their fortune yet still dream of cruisin' à la *American Graffiti*. With the flame motif blazing back from the hood and state-of-the-art mechanics below it, this baby is ready to burn up any street in the nation.

Ted Drewes has provided an Arctic refuge for overheated residents of St. Louis, Missouri, since 1929. The family's private custard recipes inspire fervent fans. Almost hot enough to thaw the icicles off Ted Drewes is this spectacular 1953 Buick Skylark. Built to celebrate Buick's fiftieth anniversary, this limited-production cherry chariot is not for the fainthearted. It features Buick's first V-8 engine and a chopped windshield, which, together with the sensationally dipped belt line, make it the automotive embodiment of a fireworks display. With a hot ride like this Buick, a cool custard stop is a necessity.

Built in 1931 and operated as a taxidermy, trading post, and tourist attraction, America's largest log cabin in Flagstaff, Arizona, was converted into a saloon in 1936 by one Doc Williams. In the 1960s and 1970s, the Museum Club's prime Route 66 location made it a venue for country music's rising and established stars, including Willie Nelson and Waylon Jennings. Like a medley of poignant and racy country tunes, immaculate vintage cars from the Route 66 Car Club cram the parking lot.

This elegant gray 1935 Duesenberg Model SSJ is the epitome of a sports car. "SS" stands for "Super-Short": the car's short wheelbase pares down the typically massive Duesenberg proportions, making this car more maneuverable in tight spots. Yet this is still a hefty automobile, with an overall weight of 5,010 pounds. Only two SSJs were ever built: Gary Cooper bought this one, prompting Clark Gable to buy the second.

Buckminster Fuller's geodesic dome is a supreme example of enclosed space created in the most efficient way possible. Years before the minivan, Fuller achieved similar results with the torpedo-shape 1934 Dymaxion Four-Door Transport. Powered by a Ford V-8 engine with a top speed of 120 mph, the Dymaxion was a rocket that never got off the ground. Of the three prototypes built, only one is known to exist.

AUGUST

Designed by Rust Heinz, scion of the famous "57 Varieties" family, the sinister 1938
Phantom Corsair featured airplane cockpit instrumentation, including an altimeter,
barometer, and compass. Undoubtedly, with those narrow windows it was easy to get lost.

1930s Chevrolet hood ornament

The unusual hood ornament on this 1930 Packard Model 7-34 Speedster Runabout is a very sculptural rendering of a young boy.

This Art Deco–inspired logo is almost a throwaway detail by the designer since it is located on the rear luggage rack of the 1932 Lincoln V-12.

AUGUST

1 2 3 4 5 6 7 8 9 10 11 12 13 14 15 16 17 18 **19** 20 21 22 23 24 25 26 27 28 29 30 31

1948 Tucker Four-Door Sedan badge

The advertising campaign for the frill-free Road Runner flaunted its austerity. Built for speed, this 1970 Plymouth Hemi Road Runner shucked chrome adornments for serious power. However, it was not without a sense of humor: its horn went "beep beep."

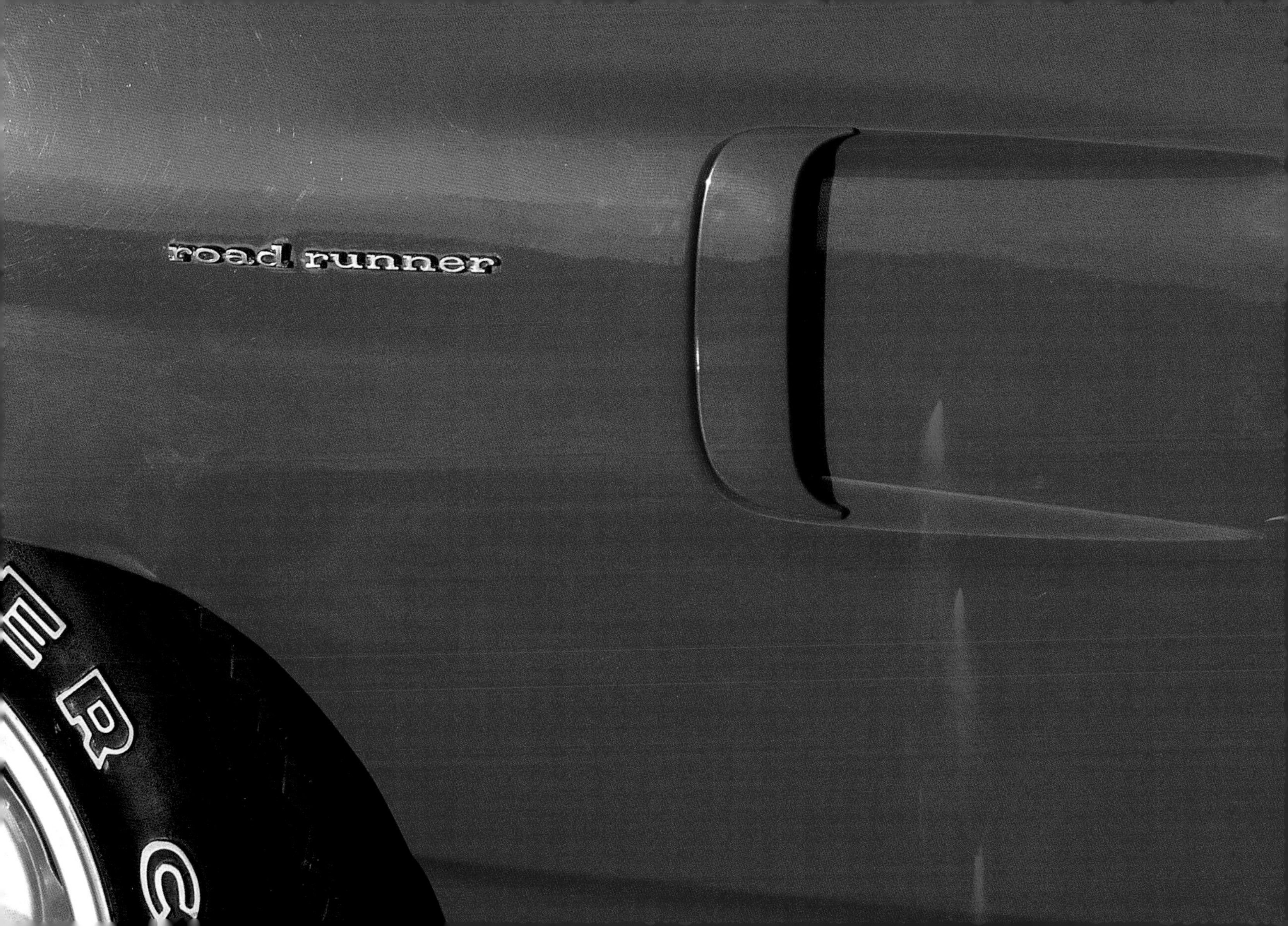
road runner

The **Z28** has always been the performance variant of the Camaro line, originally conceived as a sporty compact. For the driver who wants an extra margin of excitement, the Camaro suspension and engine modifications always seemed to do the trick.

Once Ford helped to establish the SUV market with the enormous success of the Explorer, it moved upscale with the Expedition. This larger and more luxurious vehicle succeeded in segmenting the SUV market even further.

The object of many an adolescent (and postadolescent) fantasy is this 1991 Lamborghini Diablo. The super-low-slung Lamborghini has a few things in common with visiting a shrink: it's expensive and you lie back so flat (on the richest leather seating) that your deepest feelings are bound to well up when you take off down the road. It's a bargain compared to yacht racing, which George Plimpton once described as "standing in a cold shower tearing up hundred dollar bills."

A trio of fabulous Thunderbirds cluster in the parking lot of their namesake motel in Joplin, Missouri, like guests of honor. From left to right are the 1955, 1958, and 1957 models of the famed Ford Thunderbird.

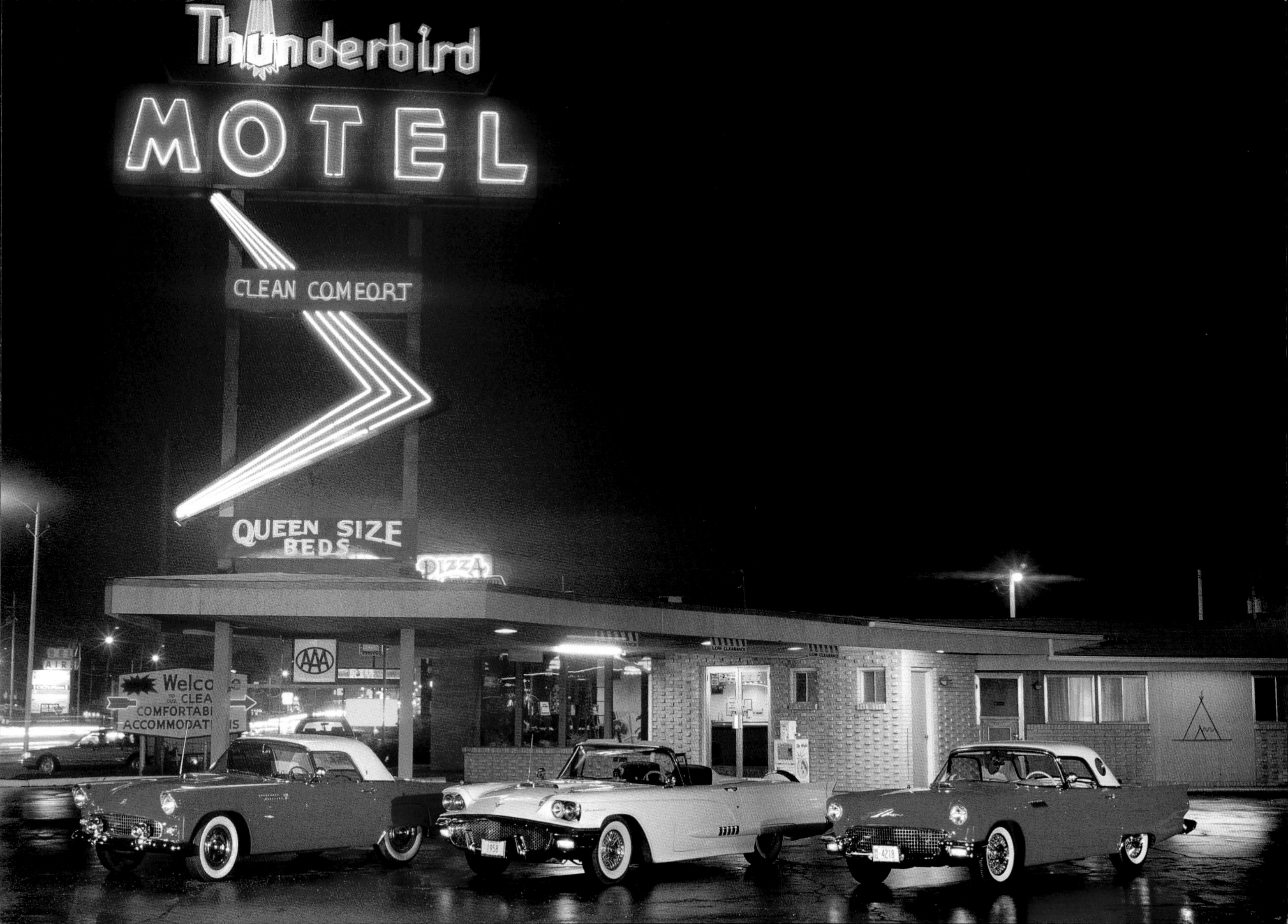
Thunderbird
MOTEL
CLEAN COMFORT
QUEEN SIZE BEDS
PIZZA

The Boots Motel in Carthage, Missouri, is a classic from the early days of motor tourism. At its 1939 opening, the Boots advertised "A Radio in Every Room" (these days, discerning readers will notice "HBO" spelled out in Gothic letters). The covered carport with every room is a reminder of a time when cars were considered a coveted luxury rather than the necessity they have become. The 1935 census listed 9,848 tourist camps across the country; by 1940 there were twenty thousand. By the time this 1955 DeSoto Firedome Sportsman came along, cars were the predominant form of travel in America. Novelty in design became key to car sales. This DeSoto was part of a much-ballyhooed "Forward Look" styling campaign. It features DeSoto's first tail fins and an arresting steel-framed wraparound windshield with optional sun-cap visor.

BOOTS
MOTEL
OFFICE
VACANCY
American Owned
Queen Bed HBO
Clean Rooms Tele

AUGUST

1 2 3 4 5 6 7 8 9 10 11 12 13 14 15 16 17 18 19 20 21 22 23 24 25 **26** 27 28 29 30 31

The vivid image of the El Vado Indian chief looms above this 1958 Ford Fairlane Skyliner Retractable Convertible Coupe like a neon sunset. Machinery necessary to convert from hardtop to let-it-all-hang-out convertible? Seven reversible electric motors, ten power relays, and twelve limit switches.

EL VADO
MOTEL
NO VACANCY

NEW MEXICO
US
66

WELCOME
KITCHENETTS
WEEKLY RATES
TV
FREE LOCAL CALLS

OFFICE

54 YEARS OF
CONTINUOUS
HOSPITALITY ON

ROUTE
66

Lest anyone think Pawtucket, Rhode Island, even a minute behind the times, the Modern Diner reminds us that the town is cutting edge. One of only two surviving examples of a Sterling Streamliner diner (and the first diner ever to be registered as a National Historic Place), the Modern catches the eye of highway drivers with its bulletlike design. The clean lines of the enamel-clad exterior suggest efficiency, reassuring travelers that they will have brisk, in-and-out service. Equally streamlined, the debonair Studebaker Commander Starlight Coupe seems to be moving even at rest. The famous "bullet-nose" front end was designer Raymond Loewy's conscious salute to the airplane, and the spectacular three-element rear window further contributes to its sleek appearance.

AUGUST

1 2 3 4 5 6 7 8 9 10 11 12 13 14 15 16 17 18 19 20 21 22 23 24 25 26 27 **28** 29 30 31

This yellow 1956 Ford Thunderbird Convertible preens in front of the Tower Theater, a recently refurbished example of a classic 1940s movie palace.

AUGUST

1 2 3 4 5 6 7 8 9 10 11 12 13 14 15 16 17 18 19 20 21 22 23 24 25 26 27 28 **29** 30 31

The El Monte Drive-In recalls the heyday of drive-in movies, when they were as much a car show as a moviegoing experience. Cars such as this 1954 Chevrolet Bel Air Coupe provided their owners with status as well as privacy for more intimate moments with their dates.

For many Corvette aficionados, model years 1963 to 1967 represent a pinnacle of styling and engineering never again equaled. What is most striking about these cars is their remarkable balance of raw sex appeal and genuine high performance. Head GM designer Bill Mitchell and his staff created a body both graceful and knife-edged (extensively refined in a wind tunnel), while head engineer Zora Arkus-Duntov ensured that the car was not just another pretty face. Fully independent suspension (rare in those days, especially for an American car), four-wheel disc brakes, and fuel injection are just a few of the advanced features of this timeless 1965 Corvette.

JACK'S LOUNGE
and PIZZA
LIQUOR
STORE
LOUNGE
Coors
ON TAP
Budweiser
CARPETS
ORIENTAL
RUGS
CORVETTE

Any cross-country trip worth its salt includes a stop for mechanical contemplation. The music of a ratcheting jack and passing cars merges with the hum of roadside crickets as we pause for adjustments. This "breakdown" is no comment on the Rambler—a great car with a thrifty six-cylinder engine and clever space utilization, a tradition soon after abandoned by Detroit but carried on by the Japanese. Perhaps this immaculate 1961 Rambler Cross Country Classic has succumbed to the lure of the jackrabbits on this stretch of road near Joseph City, Arizona. Founded by a marketing whiz who saw that Burma Shave had hit on a great idea, the Jack Rabbit Trading Post erected a long string of cryptic billboards featuring the jackrabbit against a yellow background. After miles of these images, drivers dying of curiosity welcomed the "here it is" billboard.

"As a kid, I always looked forward to our family treks from San Diego to Michigan for family reunions. . . . One particularly memorable trip took us from San Bernardino to Chicago through some of the hottest and driest country I've ever seen before or since. I don't remember the summer of 1964 being significantly hotter than any other year, but with all seven of us packed in that 1963 Rambler Classic 660 station wagon, the heat became unbearable. On the outskirts of Oklahoma City, we found our salvation . . . a $5 air-conditioner! It consisted of an ingeniously folded cardboard box that hung through the partially opened front passenger's window. The box was filled to the brim with dry ice. As the car picked up speed, outside air was forced through the opening in the front of the box across and through the dry ice. . . . We were in heaven!"

WILLIAM I. WAITE, OAK HARBOR, WASHINGTON

This 1903 Ford Model A Rear Entrance Tonneau was one of the first vehicles produced by the fledgling Ford Motor Company. Founded in 1903, Ford rocketed to worldwide fame with the success of the later Model T.

SEPTEMBER

1 **2** 3 4 5 6 7 8 9 10 11 12 13 14 15 16 17 18 19 20 21 22 23 24 25 26 27 28 29 30

Couple the modern plumbing devices of the time with the horseless buggy and you have it: the 1902 Capitol Steamer Chariot. When the steam was up, the automotive gladiator of 1902 could claim an easy speed victory at any circus (Maximus or otherwise). This lightweight chariot featured constant rear-wheel torque.

SEPTEMBER

1 2 **3** 4 5 6 7 8 9 10 11 12 13 14 15 16 17 18 19 20 21 22 23 24 25 26 27 28 29 30

One reason for the Model A's phenomenal popularity was its flexibility. Among its many iterations were milk trucks, depot hacks for toting luggage, and hearses. This rare surviving 1929 Ford Model A example hauled mail, a task perfectly suited for A's rugged dependability.

The environmentally minded Stanley Steam Cars with their quiet, almost pollution-free engines were conceived and manufactured by the twin Stanley brothers. This 1908 Stanley Steamer lightweight "racer" model was extremely fast for its day—capable of 80 mph—far too fast for most of the crude roads of the era.

SEPTEMBER

1 2 3 4 **5** 6 7 8 9 10 11 12 13 14 15 16 17 18 19 20 21 22 23 24 25 26 27 28 29 30

1959 Cadillac Fleetwood fin

SEPTEMBER

1 2 3 4 5 **6** 7 8 9 10 11 12 13 14 15 16 17 18 19 20 21 22 23 24 25 26 27 28 29 30

Tail Fin
El Reno, Oklahoma

1964 ½ Ford Mustang dashboard

SEPTEMBER

1 2 3 4 5 6 7 **8** 9 10 11 12 13 14 15 16 17 18 19 20 21 22 23 24 25 26 27 28 29 30

Flouting outrageous chrome bumpers and a stainless-steel roof, the 1957 Cadillac
Eldorado Brougham put the va-va-voom back in motoring.

SEPTEMBER

1 2 3 4 5 6 7 8 **9** 10 11 12 13 14 15 16 17 18 19 20 21 22 23 24 25 26 27 28 29 30

A true land yacht on wheels, the 1916 Crane-Simplex Touring is loaded with nautical styling cues: note the ship-styled air ducts on the car's front end and the propeller attaching the spare tire to the rear (see September 10). The unique design can be traced to Henry Crane's occupation as a builder of marine engines.

SEPTEMBER

1 2 3 4 5 6 7 8 9 **10** 11 12 13 14 15 16 17 18 19 20 21 22 23 24 25 26 27 28 29 30

1916 Crane-Simplex Touring

SEPTEMBER

1 2 3 4 5 6 7 8 9 10 **11** 12 13 14 15 16 17 18 19 20 21 22 23 24 25 26 27 28 29 30

Reminiscent of the stagecoach days of yore, this elegant 1927 Lincoln Coaching Brougham sported a wooden "coach" body with a leather-trimmed roof.

SEPTEMBER

1 2 3 4 5 6 7 8 9 10 11 **12** 13 14 15 16 17 18 19 20 21 22 23 24 25 26 27 28 29 30

1914 Simplex Speed Car

SEPTEMBER

1 2 3 4 5 6 7 8 9 10 11 12 **13** 14 15 16 17 18 19 20 21 22 23 24 25 26 27 28 29 30

The Thomas Motor Company of Buffalo, New York, rose to worldwide fame when a "sister" car to this 1907 Touring Model won the famous 1907 New York-to-Paris race. Its elegant interior fittings would have assured the owner of its extremely high quality.

1 2 3 4 5 6 7 8 9 10 11 12 13 **14** 15 16 17 18 19 20 21 22 23 24 25 26 27 28 29 30

The famed 1913 Peugeot Coupe de l'Auto took second place in the 1913 Indy 500 race and influenced engine design on almost every race car thereafter.

The gleaming body on this 1927 Vauxhall Type OE 30/98 is fashioned from aluminum.

SEPTEMBER

1 2 3 4 5 6 7 8 9 10 11 12 13 14 15 **16** 17 18 19 20 21 22 23 24 25 26 27 28 29 30

1947 Studebaker Pickup Truck

Tucumcari, New Mexico

SEPTEMBER

1 2 3 4 5 6 7 8 9 10 11 12 13 14 15 16 **17** 18 19 20 21 22 23 24 25 26 27 28 29 30

Two-Lane Blacktop
New Mexico

In 1967, T. J. Otcasek and his new bride set off for a dream honeymoon in California in their new 1967 Cadillac Eldorado:

"What better way to start our new life together? . . . About 15 miles east of Grants, [New Mexico], we came upon the most beautiful ribbons of cement we had seen so far. Blue sky, majestic mountains, new bride, new Eldo, and a ribbon of cement as far as you could see. Not too difficult to figure out now was the time to let her go (the Eldo, that is)."

T. J. OTCASEK, PUEBLO WEST, COLORADO

SEPTEMBER

1 2 3 4 5 6 7 8 9 10 **11** **12** 13 14 15 16 17 **18** 19 20 21 22 23 24 25 26 27 28 29 30

Lucille's Gas
Hydro, Oklahoma

SEPTEMBER

1 2 3 4 5 6 7 8 9 10 11 12 13 14 15 16 17 18 **19** 20 21 22 23 24 25 26 27 28 29 30

1937 Cord Model 812 Berline Limousine dashboard

SEPTEMBER

1 2 3 4 5 6 7 8 9 10 11 12 13 14 15 16 17 18 19 **20** 21 22 23 24 25 26 27 28 29 30

This back-seat bar in a 1930 Cadillac limousine is the last word in luxury. Not only were cut-crystal decanters provided as standard equipment for this mobile watering hole, so were crystal perfume atomizers that riders could use to freshen up after imbibing.

1930 Graham Paige All Weather Cabriolet interior

SEPTEMBER

1 2 3 4 5 6 7 8 9 10 11 12 13 14 15 16 17 18 19 20 21 **22** 23 24 25 26 27 28 29 30

Fast and furious may be the moniker for this 1972 AMC Javelin. The Javelin name rose to fame when race-car driver Mark Donohue drove the car to the Sports Car Club of America's 1970 Trans-Am road-racing series championship.

SEPTEMBER

1 2 3 4 5 6 7 8 9 10 11 12 13 14 15 16 17 18 19 20 21 22 **23** 24 25 26 27 28 29 30

Oldsmobile's great sales success in 1970 was due in large part to demand for the Cutlass model line. Prized Oldsmobile styling and a wide range of options at competitive prices helped place the 1970 Oldsmobile Cutlass Rallye 350 near the top of the model popularity charts.

SEPTEMBER

1 2 3 4 5 6 7 8 9 10 11 12 13 14 15 16 17 18 19 20 21 22 23 **24** 25 26 27 28 29 30

The 1998 Cadillac Evoq concept is a turn-of-the-millennium stylistic manifesto for Cadillac. With brave new styling and technological innovations such as night vision (aerospace technology that projects an image of the road onto the windshield in dark driving conditions), the Evoq signals Cadillac's determination to define the direction of cars in the twenty-first century. Cadillac's operating philosophy is "art and science"—cutting-edge research endowing American luxury cars with unparalleled technological refinement.

SEPTEMBER

1 2 3 4 5 6 7 8 9 10 11 12 13 14 15 16 17 18 19 20 21 22 23 24 **25** 26 27 28 29 30

The mechanistic design of this 1987 Lamborghini Countach is reminiscent of the evil
Death Star, bastion of power for Darth Vader of *Star Wars* fame.

The 1989 Lamborghini Anniversary edition is the crowning achievement of the Countach series. Marcello Gandini, who also penned the Countach's successor, the Diablo, designed the body. The engine, a 455-horsepower, 48-valve aluminum V-12 with two camshafts per head, manages to power the Countach to more than 180 mph.

SEPTEMBER

1 2 3 4 5 6 7 8 9 10 11 12 13 14 15 16 17 18 19 20 21 22 23 24 25 26 **27** 28 29 30

This 1996 Plymouth Prowler takes us straight back to the joy of souped-up hot rods and street racing in the 1950s. An unambiguous fun-car with sophisticated technology, the Prowler attracts attention wherever it goes. This is the car for boomers who didn't get enough *American Graffiti* the first time around.

The ultimate status symbol for flourishing American capitalists, the 1990 Ferrari F40.

One of the most coveted Porsches in recent memory, the 1988 Porsche 959 was barred from import into the United States by the Environmental Protection Agency. A loophole allowed for the importation of a few examples designed specifically for racetrack use. Hence this 959S (for sport) is one of the rarest Porsche models of recent years and a true object of 1980s desire.

SEPTEMBER

1 2 3 4 5 6 7 8 9 10 11 12 13 14 15 16 17 18 19 20 21 22 23 24 25 26 27 28 29 **30**

1988 Porsche 959S

This 1965 Mercer Cobra was a design exercise by Virgil Exner to show the many uses of copper and its alloys as automotive brightwork.

The expansive hood on this 1970 Plymouth Barracuda is interrupted by an enormous hood scoop designed to gulp air for the lightning-quick Hemi engine.

It is easy to imagine Audrey Hepburn as Sabrina looking wistfully out of the carriage-house window at this 1953 Packard Caribbean Convertible, which could well have been driven by William Holden in Billy Wilder's film *Sabrina*. The Packard is just the kind of magnificent car that would have impressed the impressionable young girl Hepburn so memorably brought to life.

1936 Duesenberg Model SJ Convertible Coupe wheel

OCTOBER

1 2 3 4 **5** 6 7 8 9 10 11 12 13 14 15 16 17 18 19 20 21 22 23 24 25 26 27 28 29 30 31

One of the coolest examples of Streamline Moderne architecture is the Coral Court Motel on Route 66 in St. Louis, Missouri. It featured a truly modern innovation: garages adjoined each room via an inner door, allowing visitors to enter and exit without scrutiny from the prying eyes of the outside world. This extra measure of privacy would make the Coral Court notorious as one of the original "no-tell" motels. After many a steamy night, alas, the Coral Court has been torn down. Every bit as sleek but a good deal more public are the snappy lines of this unforgettable 1957 Chrysler 300 two-door hardtop. Designer Virgil Exner sounded a battle cry: "Longer, Lower, Sleeker, Wider." This zesty sedan, with its wolflike tail fins, is one of his most spectacular accomplishments.

What's in the trunk of this 1960 Lincoln Mark V Convertible—a pop-up butler sporting a tray of freshly made Singapore Slings? Swanky and oversized, this Rat Pack mobile is the ideal car to impress the sharkskin suits at Trader Vic's, one of the best-known and beloved night spots in Beverly Hills.

A two-door Pontiac Grand Prix in the neon red-light district of the Sunset Strip. Note the opera window, a vintage styling motif that has passed out of favor in recent years. The window along with the rakish curve of the hood epitomize late-1970s styling. This particular model happens to be a favorite of the low-rider crowd and can be seen in modified form cruising the streets of Hollywood.

OCTOBER

1 2 3 4 5 6 7 **8** 9 10 11 12 13 14 15 16 17 18 19 20 21 22 23 24 25 26 27 28 29 30 31

Automotive designer Harley Earl was selected to design the LaSalle, a new GM division positioned to fill the price gap between the Buick and the upscale Cadillac. His final design won Earl kudos, with the fender and radiator grille clearly influenced by Hispano-Suiza designs of the day.

OCTOBER

1 2 3 4 5 6 7 8 **9** 10 11 12 13 14 15 16 17 18 19 20 21 22 23 24 25 26 27 28 29 30 31

The famous "coffin nose" of the 1937 Cord Convertible, designed by Gordon Buehrig

The sumptuous interior of the 1930 Cadillac Model 353 Berline Transformable
(custom-bodied by Hibbard et Darrin) is fitted with a plushly upholstered rear seat.

OCTOBER

1 2 3 4 5 6 7 8 9 10 **11** 12 13 14 15 16 17 18 19 20 21 22 23 24 25 26 27 28 29 30 31

The Art Deco design of the 1934 Chrysler Airflow featured a gently curving "waterfall" front grille embellished with a chrome crescendo.

One can easily imagine this car, a baby blue 1942 Packard Convertible Victoria, cruising the country-club scene. It owes its good looks to the design skills of "Dutch" Darrin.

This hot rod is a devilish departure from the practicality of other models in the Plymouth line, which was founded in 1928 as a thriftier version of Chrysler. Dedicated customizers tailor such vehicles to exacting specifications. Among other innovations are suicide doors (hinged at the back instead of the front), so called because they could be opened in a surprise maneuver to foil attackers. Hot rods like this 1934 Plymouth Customized Coupe Hi-Boy were souped up by subsequent generations for drag races like those featured in the film *American Graffiti*.

The quintessential flame paint on a 1933 Ford hot rod, customized by Boyd Coddington

With giant billboard signs, who needs maps? That was the marketing plan of Meramec Caverns promoter Les Dill, who paid for barn-side advertising on all roads in the vicinity. Also employed in the scheme were grade-school kids who got paid to post visiting cars (perhaps this 1954 Chevrolet Bel Air) with bumper stickers advertising the underground caverns, which are touted as a onetime hideout of Jesse James.

Henry Ford's automobile company grew like wildfire on the popularity of the Model T, but it almost lost its leadership position due to Ford's infamous resistance to change. The competition gained on Ford by producing models that made the words *Model T* synonymous with *old-fashioned*. At last Ford conceded to pressure and turned out the Model A, just in time for the Depression. The Model A's designer—Henry's son Edsel—included some Lincoln styling details that gave the Model A an upscale appearance despite its thrifty price tag. The Model A was an instant success; its relative austerity squared perfectly with the tough realities of the time. The Model A was available in a variety of body types, but the two-door Deluxe Phaeton shown here had a very limited production run. This was one of the first cars to feature vacuum-operated windshield wipers as standard equipment.

This elegant 1934 Packard Le Baron Runabout Speedster sports a boat tail and a V-12 engine.

From the very beginning, the Franklin Motor Car Company was associated with air-cooled engines. This 1904 Franklin Model Type B Light Tonneau is a prized example. But like steam engines, air-cooled engines were not the ultimate winner in the battle to control America's highways.

This special-bodied 1911 Rolls Royce Silver Ghost was outfitted with a custom picnic basket on the running board and a modified deck at the rear to hold its owner's hot-air-balloon basket.

OCTOBER

1 2 3 4 5 6 7 8 9 10 11 12 13 14 15 16 17 18 19 **20** 21 22 23 24 25 26 27 28 29 30 31

The white-on-white color scheme on this 1907 Thomas Touring is rather sedate, but the Thomas was something of a performance car in its day. A Thomas Flyer set a world record in 1907 by traveling 997 miles in 24 hours. The company slogan was "You Can't Go By a Thomas, So Go Buy One."

1911 Crane-Simplex 4-Passenger Tourabout

OCTOBER

1 2 3 4 5 6 7 8 9 10 11 12 13 14 15 16 17 18 19 20 21 **22** 23 24 25 26 27 28 29 30 31

Truckin'
Two Guns, Arizona

OCTOBER

Mojave Desert

Arizona

"1942. Little did we know that Route 66 and our way of life would disappear, never to return. World War II had been declared, and all the young men had either gone into the service or were expecting to go. We were two young people, married for a short time and trying to squeeze in all the adventure we could. We decided to go to California, packed up our black Ford V-8 and away we went. . . . We loved every mile and stopped at every pig-path. . . . We made it over the mountain and sailed into San Bernardino. Those beautiful palm trees and the orange groves!

This was all over fifty years ago. My darling husband died and I can no longer talk about this with him. But it is inscribed in my memory, never to fade away."

JANE S. NEAL, GREENWOOD, INDIANA

OCTOBER

In a classic case of perception versus reality, the gentlemen here look like they are in trouble. Their immaculate 1956 Ford Fairlane Club Sedan has broken down in what appears to be rattlesnake country. The reality: this theatrical sign near McLean, Texas, is no guarantee of rattlers nearby. Townspeople used to lay dead snakes across the road to discourage visitors, and the site closed in the mid-1960s. The stalwart Fairlane is good protection nonetheless: it originated many safety features, including seatbelts (a hit that outstripped Ford's supply), breakaway rear-view mirrors, and crash-proof doorlocks.

"Right out in the very middle of 'nowhere' the fan belt broke. No fan belt means: no generator, no water pump, overheated engine, [and] loss of coolant. I was able to make a temporary fan belt out of some binder twine that I had in the trunk. I won't elaborate on what it required to wind that sisal twine about ten turns around three pulleys, except to mention that we were in a blizzard at the time and those pulleys were very close to the radiator. . . . I couldn't believe it, but that twine belt held together for almost seventy miles."

ADRIAN J. GEBHART, DETROIT, MICHIGAN

Santa Rosa, New Mexico

In 1938, Arlene Donnell's Aunt Bridget took her to California as a high-school graduation gift:

"Aunt Bridget was 4'11" at full stretch, weighing ninety pounds. She was an excellent driver with a passion for big cars. She had a new four-door, bright-red De Soto, and into this we all climbed.

In the middle of the back seat was Mom (grandmother)—an ample woman—Pennsylvania Dutch background. At her feet was a massive wooden "food box" with supplies to sustain the six of us the entire trip. Mom was convinced that no food would be available in the wilds of the west, so she was prepared to feed us. I marvel at the amount of stuff she managed to cram into that wooden crate.

Somewhere in New Mexico or Arizona, there was an infestation of crickets. In order to keep them off the highway, cricket fences had been built beside the road. These were metal pens filled with crude oil or creosote. The crickets were mounded waist or shoulder high and the stench was overpowering. Now in Mom's cornucopia food box were some cantaloupes. These had ripened in the heat. The air inside that red De Soto was redolent with over-ripe cantaloupe— the outside heavy with dead crickets in oil. It was many years before I could even think about muskmelons.

The California border had a checkpoint. We were searched to be certain we carried no fruit into the state. I gladly parted with the cantaloupes. The border guard, looking into that big red De Soto filled with bleary-eyed Missourians, greeted us with 'Welcome to SUNNY California.' Mom called him all manner of Dutch names, because he had taken some of her precious vittles."

ARLENE C. DONNELL, SPRINGFIELD, MISSOURI

OCTOBER

1 2 3 4 5 6 7 8 9 10 11 12 13 14 15 16 17 18 19 20 21 22 23 24 25 **26** 27 28 29 30 31

Thunderbird Dashboard
Laguna, New Mexico

OCTOBER

1 2 3 4 5 6 7 8 9 10 11 12 13 14 15 16 17 18 19 20 21 22 23 24 25 26 **27** 28 29 30 31

The retro design of the Volkswagen New Beetle includes a bud vase, albeit plastic,
that harkens back to the cut-glass bud vases of 1920s luxury automobiles.

An early example of the SUV/minivan variant from the typical American car, the Nissan
Axxess featured a passenger-side sliding door. Unfortunately, this prescient feature did not
find wide acceptance in the mid-1980s market. Chrysler introduced the same feature in
the mid-1990s to resounding success.

OCTOBER

1 2 3 4 5 6 7 8 9 10 11 12 13 14 15 16 17 18 19 20 21 22 23 24 25 26 27 28 **29** 30 31

Urban trucking first gained popularity in the early 1980s with the introduction of luxury-imbued trucks like this 1988 Chevrolet F1500 Silverado.

The 1992 850i is one of a long line of classic BMW sport coupes. A 5.0-liter V-12 delivers 296 horsepower by way of a six-speed manual transmission. You can expect to go from 0 to 60 in 6.1 seconds and enjoy the scenery at a top speed of 155 mph—before an electronic speed limiter spoils your fun.

Looking a bit like a three-wheeled goldfish, this 1937 Airomobile Sedan was an air-cooled prototype designed by former Franklin automobile engineers. On a cross-country promotional tour, the car was driven almost 45,000 miles, averaging 43 mph! However, even this sensational economical performance could not help the Airomobile arrange financing in the throes of the Depression.

This red 1949 Ford Coupe hot rod is a sizzling interpretation of an automotive classic. After World War II a fast-moving automotive marketplace dictated a new challenge: cars that were faster, lower, and sleeker. Ford's answer was the 1949 Ford. Its "envelope" body changed the face of American cars and proved a runaway hit. More than any other car, this widely affordable Ford signaled the beginning of the postwar economic boom and the mass suburban migration.

NOVEMBER

1 **2** 3 4 5 6 7 8 9 10 11 12 13 14 15 16 17 18 19 20 21 22 23 24 25 26 27 28 29 30

It's a red-hot night at the El Monte. Hot-rodders would often congregate at drive-ins like this one to show off their latest creations. This state-of-the-art 1946 Ford Convertible customized by Boyd Coddington is right at home.

El Monte
EL MONTE
DRIVE-IN THEATRE
SHOW STARTS AT DUSK
HOT RODS FROM HELL
GIANT

NOVEMBER

1 2 **3** 4 5 6 7 8 9 10 11 12 13 14 15 16 17 18 19 20 21 22 23 24 25 26 27 28 29 30

Deep in Philadelphia lies the birthplace of the world-famous Philly cheese steak. Geno's is a key purveyor of the best examples of the genre. This 1959 Chevrolet Impala was significantly larger than preceding models in keeping with concurrent public taste. The Impala is distinguished by its "batmobile" fins: reviewers have commented that the rear deck is "big enough to land a Piper Cub."

NOVEMBER

1 2 3 **4** 5 6 7 8 9 10 11 12 13 14 15 16 17 18 19 20 21 22 23 24 25 26 27 28 29 30

The triumvirate of road power parked in front of the Bendix Diner in Hasbrouck Heights, New Jersey, runs the gamut from a 1950s classic to an early 1970s road-burner. From left to right, they are a 1971 Plymouth Valiant Duster 340 Coupe, a 1950 Ford Convertible, and a 1967 Pontiac Grand Prix. Their owners might be chowing down on classic diner specialties or innovations like the Chili Fiesta and Disco Fries (served with melted American cheese and gravy).

The vibrant Metro Diner is a neon Mecca in downtown Tulsa, Oklahoma. The Metro's credo of home cooking draws loyal customers from far and wide with its famous meringue pies and "'50s Faves" such as chicken pot pie and meatloaf. Looking a little like desserts, these Nash Metropolitans are almost cute enough to eat. Produced by the American Motor Corporation between 1954 and 1962, the Nash has a tiny body powered by a 1,500-cubic-inch, four-cylinder engine designed specifically for "neighborhood driving" and was ahead of its time in anticipating the 1970s trend toward fuel economy. Left to right, these models hail from 1957, 1959, 1960, 1961, and 1962.

NOVEMBER

1 2 3 4 5 **6** 7 8 9 10 11 12 13 14 15 16 17 18 19 20 21 22 23 24 25 26 27 28 29 30

This modest, all-American hot-dog stand is the setting for a 1957 Chrysler 300C convertible that represents the best of late-fifties styling. The elegantly swooped fins and tastefully shaped grille make the car a model of restraint in an era of overkill.

Though built after the heyday of the Mother Road, the Route 66 Diner in Albuquerque, New Mexico, commemorates the days when the town was an oasis for travelers making the long desert trek. The diner's top-notch Blue Plate Special and other menu delights make it a worthy successor to Sam's classic 66 Service Station, which used to occupy its place. One of the cars Sam would have serviced is this 1957 Thunderbird (right), Ford's answer to the European sports cars GIs fell for while serving abroad. This model includes a radio whose volume changes with the car's speed to compensate for wind noise—a musical version of cruise control. Raymond Loewy's design for the 1960 Studebaker Hawk (left) takes the Thunderbird's lines into the jet age. Aircraft styling influenced Loewy's jaunty tail fins, reflecting America's passion for rocket-inspired design.

NOVEMBER

1 2 3 4 5 6 7 **8** 9 10 11 12 13 14 15 16 17 18 19 20 21 22 23 24 25 26 27 28 29 30

1957 Chevrolet Bel Air

"Out past the cornfields where the woods got heavy.

Out in the back seat of my '60s Chevy.

Workin' on mysteries without any clues.

Workin' on our night moves.

Tryin' to make some front-page drive-in news.

Workin' on our night moves.

In the summertime. The sweet summertime."

FROM BOB SEGER'S SONG "NIGHT MOVES"

For many, the proportions of the 1957 Chrysler 300C tail fin are absolutely perfect.
The fin became larger and more chrome-laden in the following years, reaching its
ultimate height in 1959.

NOVEMBER

1 2 3 4 5 6 7 8 9 **10** 11 12 13 14 15 16 17 18 19 20 21 22 23 24 25 26 27 28 29 30

Winner of *Motor Trend* magazine's "Car of the Year" award, the 1968 Pontiac GTO's all-new design combined blistering performance with a full-size body.

NOVEMBER

1 2 3 4 5 6 7 8 9 10 **11** 12 13 14 15 16 17 18 19 20 21 22 23 24 25 26 27 28 29 30

Pontiac was traditionally a step up from Chevrolet in the GM pecking order, so an extra helping of chrome slathered over the bulbous flanks of this 1951 Pontiac Chieftain Eight Deluxe Convertible Coupe is no surprise. By early in the decade Pontiac sales were surging, thanks to a booming American economy.

Looking every inch like a hornet in flight, this yellow-and-black 1970 Oldsmobile Cutlass 442 W-30 hovers near Madam Sophia the palm reader.

This 1950 Dodge Coronet features the "Gyromatic Drive" option that eliminates the need for changing gears (although the car can be driven as a standard shift too). Beginning in 1949, the Coronet was the top of the line for Dodge's first all-new series of cars in the postwar era.

Ed Rexius reminisces about past road trips:

"It seemed so much more interesting to travel on those routes and stay in the small motels along the way, and stop at those old country restaurants than it does now on all those interstate highways. In those days, you would drive through all those small towns. And now you don't even know you go by them except to exit. You may get there a little quicker, but you don't get to see the real America as we did back then. Yes things were simpler and slower then."

ED REXIUS, SAGINAW, MICHIGAN

NOVEMBER

1 2 3 4 5 6 7 8 9 10 11 12 13 **14** 15 16 17 18 19 20 21 22 23 24 25 26 27 28 29 30

Acclaimed Chrysler automotive designer Virgil Exner helped Plymouth shake off its stodgy reputation with a completely new look in 1955. Two-tone paint was used very effectively as a design element, helping to emphasize the propulsive, lunging-forward look. Even better, the arrival of Plymouth's first V-8 engine backed up the crisp new styling found in this lovely 1955 Belvedere convertible. Orange Cocktails in central California features the billiards game of snooker, popularized in movies such as *The Hustler* and *The Color of Money,* which attracts professional players from across the country in high-stakes tournaments to this very day.

The 1957 Bel Air was the top-of-the-line Chevrolet. With a powerful new V-8 engine and the vastly popular Powerglide automatic transmission, the Bel Air was a mechanical leap forward from previous models. This particular Bel Air has its original Dusk Pearl and India Ivory paint job and is loaded with factory options, including electric windshield wipers, an electric clock, and front and rear bumper guards. Angled over Route 66 like a series of stylized peaks from a distant mountain range, the roof of the Galaxy Diner harkens back to the glory days of diner architecture. Though part of a franchise chain, the Galaxy Diner has a distinctive look that gives it real personality and offers a warm welcome to visitors of Flagstaff, Arizona, the "gateway to the Grand Canyon." In Flagstaff, as well as in countless other towns, Route 66 was Main Street. The vibrant town center survived the decertification of Route 66 due to the undying enthusiasm of local merchants and residents.

In the wake of the 1980s, some American automotive design has returned to a 1950s design vocabulary, spun with a uniquely 1990s sense of irony. In his 1992 Chezoom Streetrod, hot-rod builder Boyd Coddington signaled the way forward with rear fins that pay affectionate homage to the 1957 Chevy Bel Air yet with a playful, larger-than-life attitude that might be termed postmodern.

With dual intercoolers and a dual turbo, the engine of this 1985 Ferrari GTO exemplifies the ambition of the decade. One could imagine Gordon Gecko from the movie *Wall Street* revving the twelve cylinders beneath this hood.

The deeply ridged flanks of this 1986 Ferrari Testarossa look like they could stabilize a jet. Featuring consummate Ferrari engineering, the Testarossa was dressed up in a flashy skin that epitomized the 1980s era of conspicuous consumption portrayed by Tom Wolfe in *Bonfire of the Vanities*. Tricked out in Nancy Reagan red, this Ferrari commands total attention wherever it goes, tempting some to call it the "Testosterossa."

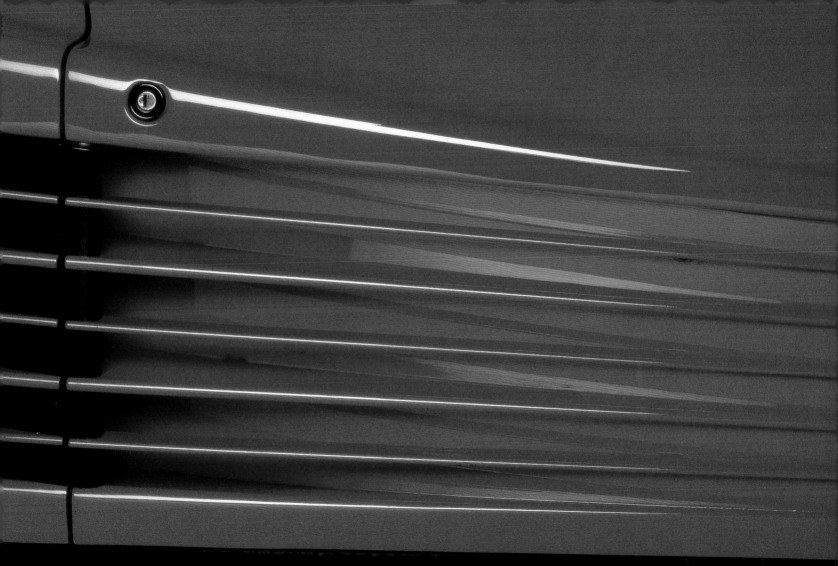

NOVEMBER

1 2 3 4 5 6 7 8 9 10 11 12 13 14 15 16 17 18 **19** 20 21 22 23 24 25 26 27 28 29 30

In 1964, Lee Iacocca and Ford made history with the introduction of the Mustang.
Chevrolet was hot on their heels with the 1967 Chevrolet Camaro SS Convertible that
emulated the basic "pony-car" formula of long hood, short deck, and big engine.

A stretch of the original Route 66 roadbed in Oklahoma shows signs of returning to the grassland it once was.

"It was 1927 and my adventurous parents were busy planning to drive our 1926 Oldsmobile from Oklahoma City to Santa Monica in June. There were no highway maps as we know them. Directions were published by auto clubs. . . . These diagrams showed mileage and landmarks, such as 'at twenty-seven miles turn right at the white school house.'

On the appointed day the four of us, which included me at fourteen and my brother eight years younger, set out. Pavement was largely reserved for cities. Our first ten miles were paved; the next hard surface would be 280 miles away at Amarillo. . . . Asphalt had replaced the old plank road through the sands of the Mojave Desert. . . . This was a disappointment since I would have relished the excitement of riding the planks. These were scarcely wide enough to accommodate a car. Should you have the misfortune of letting a wheel go over the edge, other drivers would have to lift you back in order to continue their journey.

An innovation for auto travelers had arisen—the 'tourist camp.' These generally were comprised of a dozen single-walled frame cabins with one or two double beds, renting for $1.00 or $1.50, respectively. These had no bedding, only mattresses. We carried ours in duffel bags lashed to the car's running boards. A latrine for all guests was placed in the middle of the camp. Water was supplied by a spigot at the door of each cabin. Sometimes a gas or kerosene plate was available for cooking. The final amenity was a broom. This almost always had to be used before unpacking since the former occupant had been too rushed to perform the task."

ROBERT C. SCOTT, LOS ANGELES, CALIFORNIA

NOVEMBER

1 2 3 4 5 6 7 8 9 10 11 12 13 14 15 16 17 18 19 20 **21** 22 23 24 25 26 27 28 29 30

Cadillac's relationship with Italian designers began with the 1959 and 1960 limited-production Eldorados built by Bertone. In the 1980s, Cadillac contracted Pininfarina to design and build the sleek two-seat body of the Cadillac Allante to compete against the Mercedes SL class. But the flagship GM vehicle failed to win back the luxury sports-car market from the Germans, further damaging GM's prestige.

With a few notable exceptions (Honda being one), automakers find small cars a hard sell in America. Ford had high hopes for the German-engineered 1988 Festiva due to its outstanding handling and sprightly acceleration. Unfortunately, in the 1980s small was not necessarily desirable, at least in the United States. In Europe, however, the Festiva was a best-seller.

NOVEMBER

1 2 3 4 5 6 7 8 9 10 11 12 13 14 15 16 17 18 19 20 21 22 **23** 24 25 26 27 28 29 30

A & W Root Beer
Visalia, California

NOVEMBER

1 2 3 4 5 6 7 8 9 10 11 12 13 14 15 16 17 18 19 20 21 22 23 **24** 25 26 27 28 29 30

Volkswagen Beetle
Yucatán, Mexico

NOVEMBER

1 2 3 4 5 6 7 8 9 10 11 12 13 14 15 16 17 18 19 20 21 22 23 24 **25** 26 27 28 29 30

Roy's Café, Motel, and Gas
East of Barstow, California

NOVEMBER

1 2 3 4 5 6 7 8 9 10 11 12 13 14 15 16 17 18 19 20 21 22 23 24 25 **26** 27 28 29 30

Stations like KNGS in California's Central Valley have always been a home for subversive, road-burning tunes like the ones that fueled this 1970 Plymouth Hemi Road Runner through many a flaming drag race.

NOVEMBER

1 2 3 4 5 6 7 8 9 10 11 12 13 14 15 16 17 18 19 20 21 22 23 24 25 26 **27** 28 29 30

Detroit's dream of putting two cars in every garage (or barn) was a powerful vision to
drive automotive sales. It also helped develop the concept of market segmentation,
which called for cars particularized to drivers' needs. This 1953 Chrysler New Yorker
Town & Country Wagon is equally adept at ferrying children or the occasional bale of hay.

Owner-friendly features made this eight-cylinder 1930 Packard 7-45 Roadster very popular. The driver's seat was easily adjustable, and the aft storage compartment provided plenty of room for luggage or golf bags. A model like this cost $4,585, almost enough (at the time) for a rather nice home.

Chrysler was an endangered company on the edge of dissolution in the late 1980s. This 1992 Dodge Viper RT/10 represents its audacious attempt to stage the return of the classic American sports car as well as bolster its chances of corporate survival. The gambit paid off: the sensational showpiece drew the public back to Chrysler showrooms. Hence the Viper's sting spurred the company's recovery.

The air scoop for the awesome Hemi engine under the hood of a 1970 Plymouth Road Runner

Wheel from a 1925 Franklin Sport Runabout. The wheel has evolved from the cart to the bicycle, the horseless carriage to the automobile, each innovation building upon its predecessor's successes and solutions. Wooden wheels from wagons and carts acquired balloon tires from bicycle designers. The resulting tire/wooden wheel hybrid became the most popular production wheel until the late 1920s when metal rims came into play. Then tubeless tires, then radials. The newest thinking involves solid or so-called airless tires. And the wheel rolls on.

1 **2** 3 4 5 6 7 8 9 10 11 12 13 14 15 16 17 18 19 20 21 22 23 24 25 26 27 28 29 30 31

Although some might call it cheating, western farmers pestered by too many coyotes took advantage of the extra horsepower of this 1928 Oakland Sports Roadster to hunt down the animals on their vast ranches.

In 1902, water was the dominant medium for cooling a car engine. It still is. But H. H. Franklin and engineer John Wilkinson thought they had a better idea—air. The Franklin Motor Company produced only air-cooled engines from 1902 until its demise in 1934. The stately design of this 1924 Franklin Series 10C was an attempt by the company to reassure a public skeptical of this unusual method. Pioneering aviators Charles Lindbergh and Amelia Earhart understood well the physics of air-cooling, and they favored the Franklin. However, it was all a lost cause: eventually, Franklin was forced to cobble on a fake radiator in order to placate the customer. This model features wooden wheels and frame with an aluminum body.

DECEMBER

Clearly the envy of its 1950s counterpart across the way, this white 1962 Chevrolet Impala Super Sport Convertible serenely enjoys its status as the happening ride at the Dog 'n' Suds. Increasing horsepower became a marketing angle in the early 1960s, and the Impala offered one of the highest performance engines in Chevy history (409 cubic inches, 425 horsepower). *Low* and *wide* were the operative words for design of this period in mercurial Detroit, with the chrome-laden bulk of the 1950s already a distant memory.

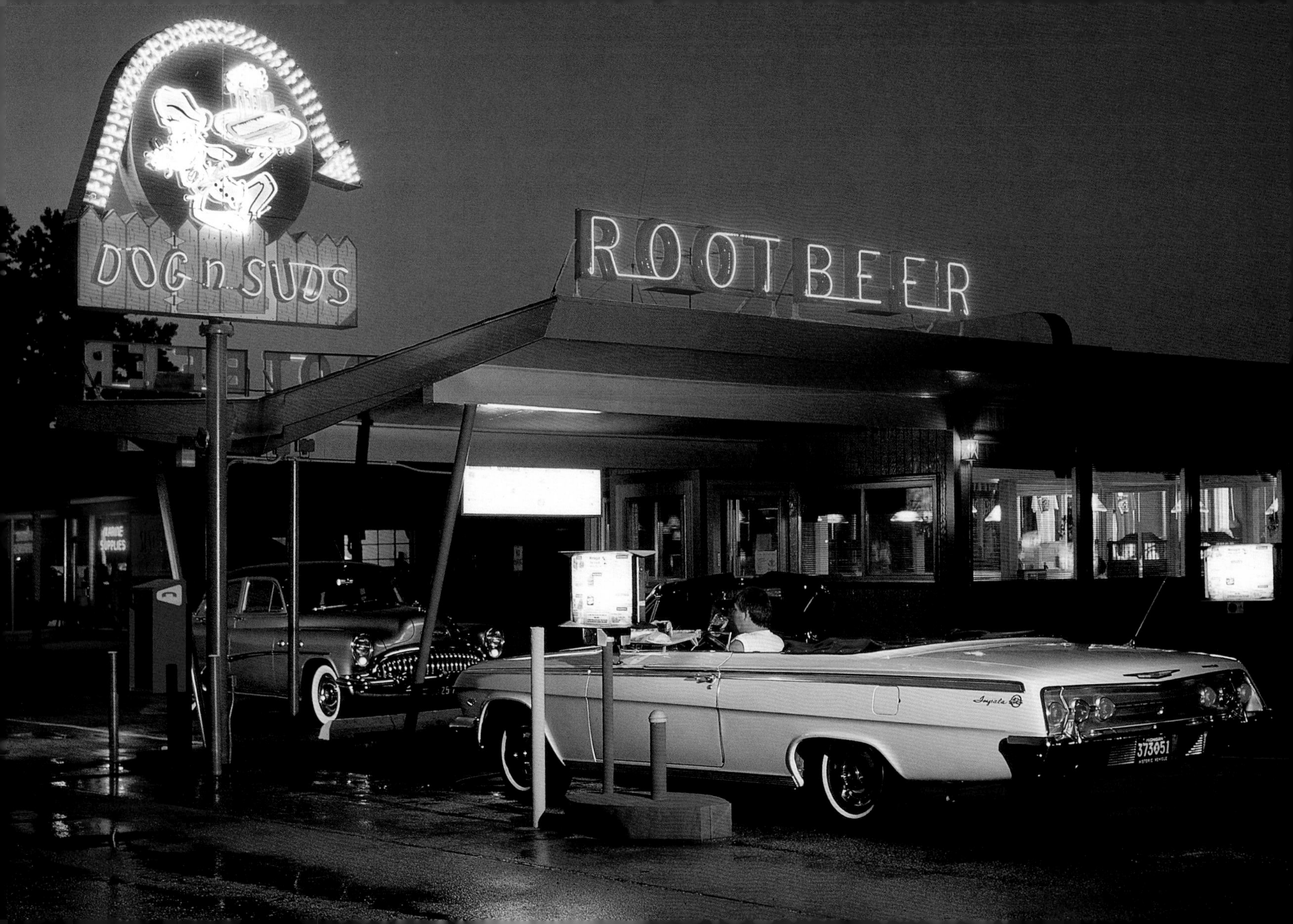
DOG n SUDS
ROOTBEER
Impala

DECEMBER

1 2 3 4 **5** 6 7 8 9 10 11 12 13 14 15 16 17 18 19 20 21 22 23 24 25 26 27 28 29 30 31

Surrounded by a swarm of finned beauties from the 1950s and 1960s, the Elgin Diner is the place to eat in Camden, New Jersey. The silver 1961 Plymouth Suburban Wagon is a particularly amazing specimen. Built at a time when Chrysler design stylist Virgil Exner was mandating the "Forward Look," this car features bizarre "twin-pod" instrumentation panels and a square Lucite steering wheel. Purchased by its current owners in 1961, the Elgin still serves the best of food with the best of service to all drivers, vintage of car notwithstanding.

DECEMBER

Henry Ford built the "999" as an experimental racer in 1902. As one of America's earliest automotive tinkerers, Ford explored a number of engineering concepts on his own before forming the Ford Motor Car Company. Barney Oldfield, a famous race-car driver of the era, drove this car to victory over the famous Winton Bullet in 1903. Later, with Henry Ford behind the wheel (or *tiller,* as it was then called), the car broke the land speed record at 91 mph on Michigan's frozen Lake St. Clair.

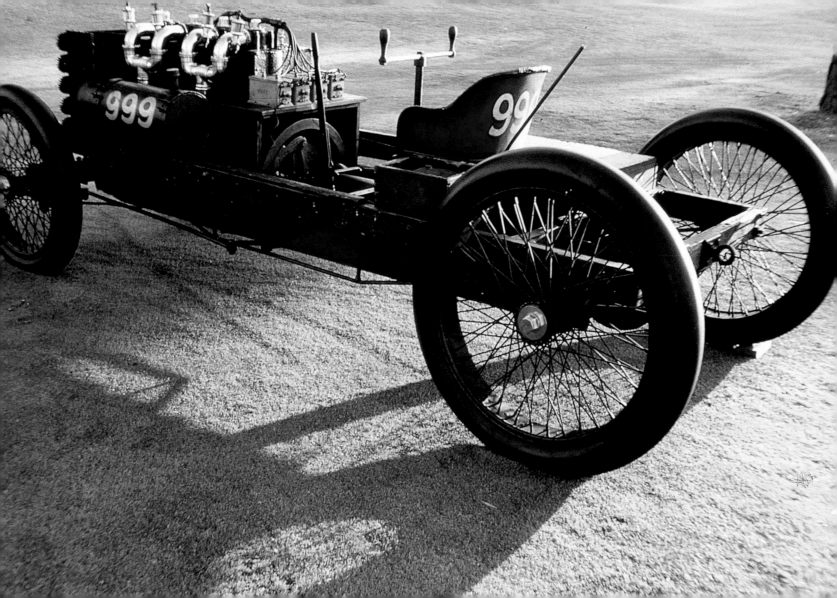

DECEMBER

1 2 3 4 5 6 **7** 8 9 10 11 12 13 14 15 16 17 18 19 20 21 22 23 24 25 26 27 28 29 30 31

At first glance, many automotive enthusiasts may identify this automobile as a Stutz Bearcat by its distinctive oval monocle windscreen. However, few know that the windscreen made its first appearance on the limited-production 1910 Marion Special Roadster when Harry Stutz was factory manager and chief engineer.

DECEMBER

1 2 3 4 5 6 7 **8** 9 10 11 12 13 14 15 16 17 18 19 20 21 22 23 24 25 26 27 28 29 30 31

Looking a bit like a horse and buggy sans the horse, this 1900 Packard Runabout is the only one of the five built that is known to still exist.

One of the few Asian restaurants along Route 66, the Grand Canyon Cafe has been owned and operated by the same family since its founding in 1938. Its specialty of American chop suey has galvanized many a traveler to press on for the nearby Grand Canyon. Barely pausing for a refuel, this 1955 Lincoln Capri is a speedster in luxury duds. By the 1950s, Lincoln had moved away from its country-club origins to the thrills of open-road racing. Lincoln dominated the legendary Carrera Panamericana road races between 1952 and 1954 but suffered from staid styling left over from its white-shoe days. The button-down duckling became a speed swan with the restyled Lincoln Capri, whose tighter lines reflected its road-racing capabilities and left the polo-and-tennis crowd eating dust.

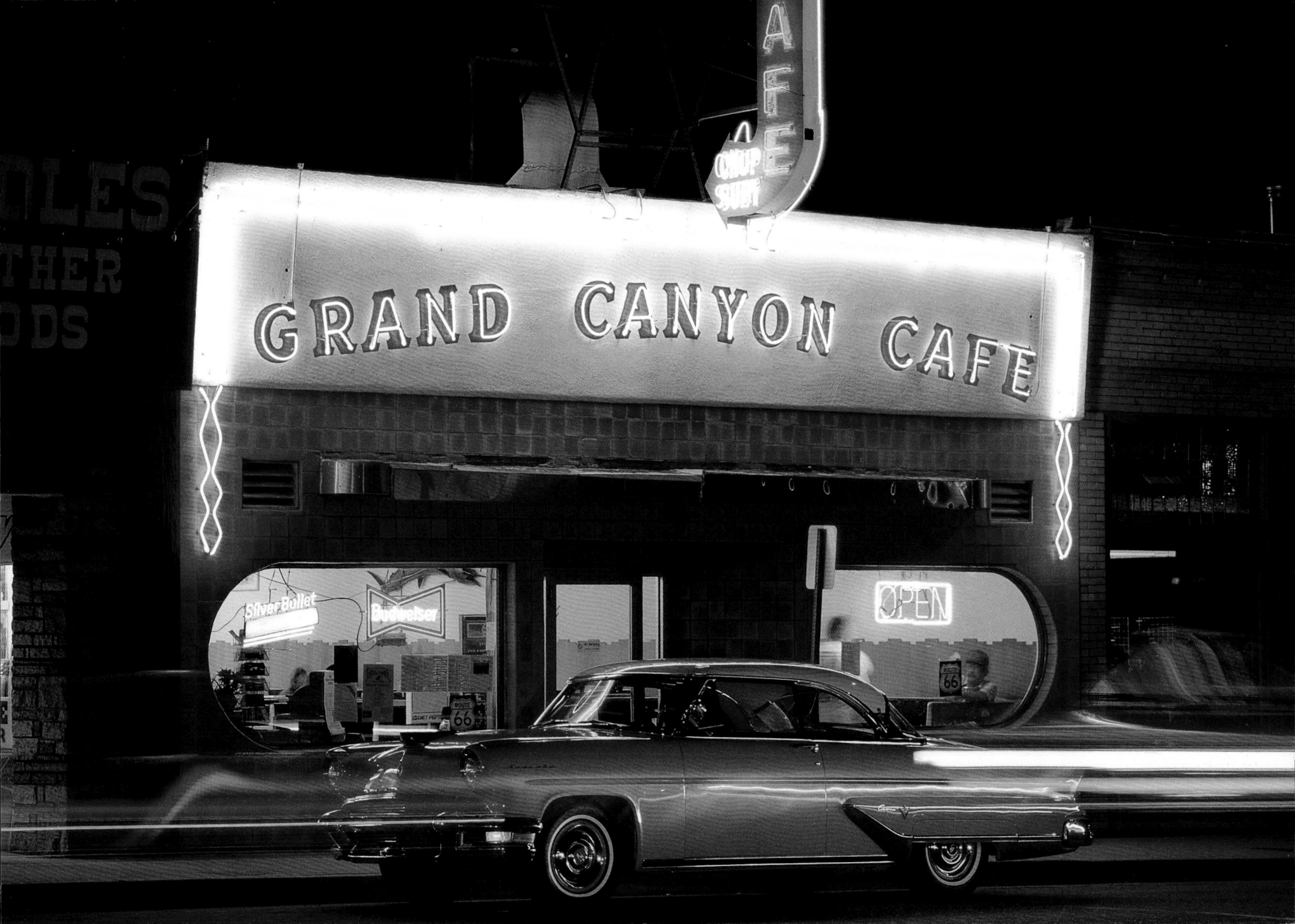
GRAND CANYON CAFE
Silver Bullet
Budweiser
OPEN
ROUTE 66

DECEMBER

1 2 3 4 5 6 7 8 9 **10** 11 12 13 14 15 16 17 18 19 20 21 22 23 24 25 26 27 28 29 30 31

Located at the Texan "Crossroads of America" (where Route 66 crosses Mexico-to-Canada Route 83), the U Drop Inn Cafe was built in 1936 as a meeting place for local ranchers. These two sedans, a 1956 Chevrolet Bel Air and a 1955 Ford Fairlane, are right at home. With their solid construction and pleasing pastel paint jobs these sedans are the kind of upstanding workhorses that ferried Texas citizens across the plains at the time the classic film *Giant* hit the screen. With James Dean, Rock Hudson, and Elizabeth Taylor, George Stevens's *Giant,* adapted from Edna Ferber's novel, made Texas the backdrop for an unforgettable American drama.

DECEMBER

The 1919 Ford Model T Touring is an American classic, one of the most popular family cars of all time.

"My experience dates back to 1920, at which time I was twelve years old. Our family transportation was limited to streetcars and trains. My father reached the point in his life where he thought we should have some family transportation. His choice was a 1920 Harley Davidson motorcycle with a sidecar attached. Mother's seat was in the sidecar. Brother Dick sat on a little stool between Mother's sprattled legs, which left his head just a little above the front panel of the sidecar. My seat was on a tandem behind my father.

Dad had rigged up a luggage carrier on the back of the sidecar, which accommodated picnic food and a small propane gas stove. Food never tasted so good!

On one memorable trip to Eureka, we experienced a flat tire on the rear of the motorcycle. Removing the rear wheel and repairing the puncture bordered on a major project, and I think it was responsible for my Dad making up his mind to trade the motorcycle for a shiny new 1925 Chevrolet sedan."

ART J. MUELLER, ST. LOUIS, MISSOURI

DECEMBER

1 2 3 4 5 6 7 8 9 10 11 **12** 13 14 15 16 17 18 19 20 21 22 23 24 25 26 27 28 29 30 31

Even today, cruising America's highways behind the wheel of this fabulous 1941 Cadillac Series 60 Special is a special treat.

The solid construction of Cadillacs made them popular for traversing the long distances of the American West as well as the civilized boulevards back East. This 1941 Cadillac Series 60 was a stout ship for the uncharted waters west of the Mississippi.

DECEMBER

1 2 3 4 5 6 7 8 9 10 11 12 13 **14** 15 16 17 18 19 20 21 22 23 24 25 26 27 28 29 30 31

Chrysler

Fancy Town, North Carolina

Onward

Route 66, Arizona

Constance Rimkus and her family had to cross the Mojave Desert in 1940:

"We had to cross it and it was hot as *%&*#>. There was a big sign that said 'Fill your gas tank here. Last station before going through the desert.' So we stopped and filled the tank and after that asked the attendant if we all could have a glass of water. We were so thirsty and it was so hot! He said, 'Sure, for twenty-five cents a glass, you can drink all you want.' We went into total shock. We asked, 'You're charging us for water? You can't do that, water is free!' He said, 'Oh yes I can. Do you see any other place around here where you can get any water?'

Of course not. We were virtually in the middle of nowhere. Not another house or barn or store could be seen anywhere. He reminded us that we might have a flat tire and the strength to change it could make people faint. Plus he also reminded us we should carry water on the front of the car in a canvas bag to cool the hot air blowing across the radiator. So all in all he got us for quite a bundle. Oh yes, he also sold us a thermos bottle full of water. His parting words to us were, 'I hope you folks make it. So many don't, ya know.'"

CONSTANCE M. RIMKUS, HICKORY HILLS, ILLINOIS

Busted

Arizona

Yves Bolomet writes about his 1956 two-week leave from the Air Force radio school before being shipped overseas. He was driving a 1956 Chevy Bel Air to his home in Los Angeles when he came upon a less-than-courteous driver who crawled along the curves and sped up on the straights so that at first Mr. Bolomet couldn't pass him. But he finally did, and this is what happened:

"I had just started to get back to the rhythm of the road, when I saw the flashing red light of a New Mexico Highway Patrol car. Despite my pleas, we drove off together to see the judge in his combination courthouse and curio store. After a steep and unpayable fine had been assessed, I was carted off to the Las Lunas County jail.

By the time the sheriff reached my father, I had taught the local inmates the basics of seven-card stud, more or less learned how to roll Bull Durham, and learned to love a diet of soft-boiled eggs, Wonder bread, and hot, hot, hot peppers. When I finally got out, nearly a week later, the judge relented somewhat and gave me some really nice turquoise jewelry along with his best wishes."

YVES BOLOMET, SYLMAR, CALIFORNIA

DECEMBER

1 2 3 4 5 6 7 8 9 10 11 12 13 14 15 16 **17** 18 19 20 21 22 23 24 25 26 27 28 29 30 31

A consistent winner in the intermediate car ranks, this 1972 Chevrolet Malibu Convertible provided trim yet spacious transportation. By today's standards, the car is full size, but in the era of big cars, the Malibu fell into the midsize ranks. The gasoline crisis of the early 1970s finished off production of these last muscle cars in favor of more thrifty compact cars.

To drive into the future in cars such as this 1959 Edsel Corsair Convertible, we needed modern four-lane highways with banked curves and EZ-On and EZ-Off exits. While the new freeways were being built, we fumed along behind slowpokes on our woefully inadequate two-lane roads. All that V-8 power and nowhere to really open it up! Opportunities to pass were eagerly awaited.

Anna Avellino headed to California from New Jersey in 1959 to be with her married daughter and grandchildren. She writes about her "life in the fast lane" experiences:

"We were in a row of five or six cars following a slow truck up a hill. One by one, each car pulled over and passed, so I did the same, only to find a policeman over the hill. He pulled us all over and gave us tickets and directed us to a shack set up like a court and fined us $15 each. I believe this was a tourist trap."

ANNA AVELLINO, HESPERIA, CALIFORNIA

During the 1960s, the Big Three automakers marketed two different product lines. On the one hand, they tried to sell the consumer on more economical, compact cars, but on the other hand, their fascination with horsepower grew unabated. Even the mass-marketed pony cars that trotted onto the scene had names evocative of speed, such as Mustang and Firebird. This 1968 Ford Mustang Cobra Jet 428 was one of the fastest on the street.

DECEMBER

1 2 3 4 5 6 7 8 9 10 11 12 13 14 15 16 17 18 19 **20** 21 22 23 24 25 26 27 28 29 30 31

The Chevelle was positioned between the full-size Impala and the compact Nova, and perhaps combined the best of both worlds. This 1968 Chevrolet Chevelle SS 396 was small enough to maneuver easily but offered the same engine options as its big brothers.

DECEMBER

1 2 3 4 5 6 7 8 9 10 11 12 13 14 15 16 17 18 19 20 **21** 22 23 24 25 26 27 28 29 30 31

This 1966 Shelby GT 350 materializes like a ghost against the darkening sky above the Santa Monica Pier. Located at the western terminus of Route 66, the pier projects into the Pacific Ocean like "The End" at the conclusion of a great novel.

DECEMBER

1 2 3 4 5 6 7 8 9 10 11 12 13 14 15 16 17 18 19 20 21 **22** 23 24 25 26 27 28 29 30 31

Cruising for burgers in a 1958 Chevrolet Impala Sport Coupe

Neon and the open road share a common history. More than just illuminated advertising, neon signage relieves the monotony of the open road. Modest examples such as this donut shop in Joplin, Missouri, are a mere prelude to the symphonic form of roadside art in America—Las Vegas neon at night.

One of the early examples of the Oldsmobile Toronado, this 1969 model was part of the effort to integrate front-wheel drive into Oldsmobile's lineup. Big, full-size Oldsmobiles were used to announce a major departure from GM's previous disdain for front-wheel drive.

Ever since the owners of this once-humble trading post struck piping-hot mineral water
(112 degrees) while sinking a well in 1939, the Buckhorn Baths in Mesa, Arizona,
has beckoned privileged types intent on benefiting from the healthful waters. The San
Francisco Giants baseball team, for example, made the Buckhorn its health spa for
twenty-five years. What luminaries might have driven these three phenomenal vehicles to
the Buckhorn? It is hard not to think of Marilyn Monroe when noticing the outrageous tail
fins of the 1959 Cadillac Coupe DeVille (left). The 1940 Packard 110 Convertible Coupe
(center) is an example of an upscale brand that successfully adapted itself to a middle-
class audience—Lana Turner, perhaps, or maybe Betty Grable? The elegant 1931 LaSalle
Model 345A Convertible Coupe (right) won plaudits for designer Harley Earl, who was
inspired by the lines of the famous Hispano-Suiza—somebody who wanted to keep a low
profile, such as Greta Garbo?

DECEMBER

1 2 3 4 5 6 7 8 9 10 11 12 13 14 15 16 17 18 19 20 21 22 23 24 25 **26** 27 28 29 30 31

By the end of the 1950s, aspects of popular culture such as roadside neon signs were targeted by critics as "trash." The good-taste mavens were even massacring car design. Under criticism, Detroit backed off from the fin mania that peaked at the end of the decade, as exemplified in this 1959 DeSoto Firesweep Convertible Coupe.

DECEMBER

1 2 3 4 5 6 7 8 9 10 11 12 13 14 15 16 17 18 19 20 21 22 23 24 25 26 **27** 28 29 30 31

If ignited, the tail fins on this 1959 Dodge Royal Lancer Coupe might rocket you to the moon.

DECEMBER

Like a hungry hound, this 1961 Imperial Crown Convertible seems to crouch outside this neat little café hoping for a morsel to be tossed from the kitchen. Faced with constant competition from the better-known Cadillacs and Lincolns of the world, the luxury Imperial struggled to stake out its own stylistic identity. Imperial succeeded with this 1961 model, which featured many radical design devices such as "classic" headlights—chrome bullets nestled in scooped-out fenders—and "gunsight" tail lamps encircled by freestanding chrome bands. With its insouciant fins and jazzy front grille (notice the hip, off-center insignia), this convertible was truly a bachelor's companion of the highest order.

Home to several restaurants over the years—the Rock Cafe and its predecessor, the Route 66 Truck Stop—is this interesting stone building on Route 66 in Stroud, Oklahoma. The paving of Route 66 left behind numerous piles of locally quarried rock offered at bargain-basement prices. The owner purchased enough stone to construct the building for a whopping $5, and the café opened for business in 1939. This 1953 Chevrolet Bel Air body style evolved from the 1950 DeLuxe Skyline but provided more window area and a lower beltline. The addition of the Powerglide transmission in 1950 made Chevrolet the first in its class to offer a fully automatic transmission. This contributed enormously to its great success. *Motor Trend* regarded the Chevrolet as "not simply being a good value, but also being a good car." Add the convertible top, and this lovely 1953 Chevrolet Bel Air is a hands-down winner.

In 1949 Ford came out with its first fully redesigned postwar car. The American motoring public was famished, having lacked a truly new model since the late 1930s. The 1949 Ford delivered in spades. Unfortunately, owners soon discovered several mechanical problems resulting from a rushed production schedule. By 1950, these problems were mostly resolved by a hardworking team under Henry Ford II: "50 ways new, 50 ways better" was the advertising slogan for that year.

DECEMBER

1 2 3 4 5 6 7 8 9 10 11 12 13 14 15 16 17 18 19 20 21 22 23 24 25 26 27 28 29 30 **31**

The racy cream-on-red paint job of this 1932 Auburn Cabriolet adds a refined finish to the raw power of the car's V-12 engine.

INDEX

Dedicated to the owners of the roadside attractions and automobiles featured in this book. Thanks for keeping the chrome polished and the neon humming. Without your efforts, the exciting phenomenon of Roadside America would not exist.

And finally, to my newest co-pilot Elizabeth Grace, I offer some driving advice. Learn when to put the pedal to the metal, never cruise in the passing lane, and whenever possible take time to enjoy the back roads of America.

About the Author

A childhood fascination with cars (and anything else that moves—airplanes, helicopters, motorcycles) inspired Lucinda Lewis to become one of the world's premier automotive photographers. Her work has appeared in numerous publications, and her books include Abrams' *Roadside America: The Automobile and the American Dream,* as well as *American Cars, Power Behind the Wheel,* and *Porsche: The Fine Art of the Sports Car.* Lewis, who is committed to preserving car culture on film, specializes in photographing the car against the backdrop of a rapidly vanishing roadside America. She presides over the world's largest automotive stock photography library, and her website, *www.cindylewisphoto.com,* is accessed by car lovers around the world. She and her husband, John Hopkins, and their daughter, Elizabeth, live in Los Angeles.

Editor: Elisa Urbanelli
Designer: Darilyn Lowe Carnes
Production Manager: Justine Keefe

Library of Congress Cataloging-in-Publication Data

Lewis, Lucinda.
  Roadside America : 365 days / Lucinda Lewis.
    p. cm.
  ISBN 0–8109–4540–1 (hardcover)
  1. Automobiles—United States–Pictorial works.
  2. Popular culture—United States.
  3. Automobile travel—United States—History.
  I. Title.

TL23.L422 2003
629.222'0973'022–dc21

2003006975

Published in 2003 by Harry N. Abrams,
Incorporated, New York.
All rights reserved. No part of the contents of
this book may be reproduced without written
permission of the publisher.

Printed and bound in Singapore

10 9 8 7 6 5 4 3 2 1

Harry N. Abrams, Inc.
100 Fifth Avenue
New York, N.Y. 10011
www.abramsbooks.com

Abrams is a subsidiary of

LA MARTINIÈRE
G R O U P E

Front cover: Al Mac's Diner, Fall River,
Massachusetts
Back cover: 1951 Mercury Station Wagon
Photographs © Lucinda Lewis

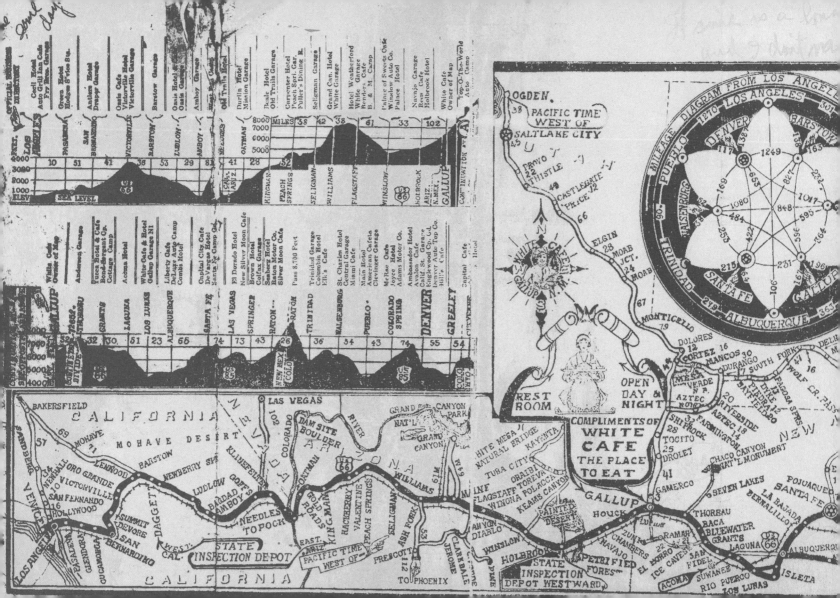